REALSIMPLE
celebrations

written by VALERIE RAINS

photographs by ANNIE SCHLECHTER

REALSIMPLE Time Inc. HOME ENTERTAINMENT

celebrate. Is there any word that evokes more promise, more joy than *celebrate?* (No, *chocolate* doesn't count, and *sleep* doesn't, either.) To truly celebrate something feels wholly good, and you usually do it with people you love—or, at the very least, don't detest. Celebrations can happen at any time and in any place, with groups large or small. In fact, some of the most memorable celebrations require no forethought and really no work at all. Genuine joy (accompanied by Champagne, of course) in the face of an engagement or a job offer or the first day of summer is better than a black-tie, petit-four extravaganza any day.

Still, life brings celebrations that inevitably require some degree of planning. And a few unenlightened souls do this math in their heads: Celebrate = party = planning + cooking + mess = oh, forget it, it's too much work. (It's sort of like that children's book *If You Give a Mouse a Cookie:* If I have a party, then I have to decide on the menu and then I have to shop and then I have to cook and then I have to clean the house and then I will be so tired that I need a nap, and when I wake up, I will be hungry and well-rested and will feel like having a party!)

The trick is to plan without actually knowing you're doing it—planned spontaneity, shall we say— and that's where *Real Simple Celebrations* comes in. The editors of *Real Simple* have done the work for you, so whether you're having Thanksgiving dinner, a baby shower, an outdoor barbecue, or anything in between, this book will give you the tools to pull it off effortlessly. Things you will find in this book*: decorating shortcuts, easy recipes, etiquette wisdom, activities for all ages, and toasts for any occasion (because, like Champagne, a good toast goes with just about anything). Things you will not find: complicated food, elaborate centerpieces, drinks you can't pronounce, or basically anything that requires a significant investment of your precious time or money.

So uncork some Champagne, kick off your shoes—because drinking Champagne in bare feet is number 17 on the list of life's greatest pleasures—and use this book to start *unplanning* your next celebration.

Kristin van Ogtrop

Managing Editor, *Real Simple*

*And if you haven't found it already, turn to the back cover. The enclosed wheel promises to take all the guesswork out of purchasing food and drink for all manner of parties. Although if you're having a party for 700, you're on your own.

from the kitchen of: *Kay Ritter*   recipe for: *A Sweet Celebration*

when: Sunday, May 15
time: 4 p.m.
place: 189 Fourth Street
r.s.v.p.: 621-322-3978

Kisses all around.
Corks pop and Champagne glasses are filled.
Guests put on party hats (and maybe lampshades).
Elizabeth and Jeff go to bed. 2-
Party starts! 8-

you're invited to a *wedding* shower
FOR   *Mary Dwight*
WHEN   *Sunday, May 19*
WHERE *Carrie's house*
TIME   *3 p.m.*
RSVP before *May 5*
by phone *311-570-2185*
by e-mail *carrie@myemail.com*

HOT DOG!

IT'S SUMMER, AND WE'RE HAVING A BARBECUE.

DATE   *Sunday, July 8*
TIME   *2 p.m. to 6 p.m.*
PLACE *the Wilsons' backyard*
       72 Ferry Lane
PLEASE BRING *A six-pack of soda and beer*

YOU'RE INVITED TO...
Humphreys Vineyard
WINE AND CHEESE PARTY
SEPTEMBER 29, 2007
5:30 P.M.

48 TEN MILE ROAD • 851-883-6907 (REGRETS ONLY)
PRODUCED AND BOTTLED BY CHARLIE AND MAGGIE HUMPHREYS

to *Casey & Greg*

say cheese

JOIN *The Thomases*
FOR WINE, CHEESE + CHATTER

WHEN *October 6th*
WHERE *172 Adams Point Road*
TIME *6 p.m.*
RSVP BEFORE *October 3rd*
BY PHONE *929-757-0074*
BY E-MAIL *thomase@myemail.com*

CELEBRATE

The Kellers
INVITE
The Hydes
TO A HOLIDAY OPEN HOUSE ON
Saturday, December 15th
4 to 8 p.m.
AT
673 Park Terrace

R.S.V.P. BEFORE *December 11th*
BY PHONE *(488) 214-1552*
BY E-MAIL *theKellers@myemail.com*

COME CELEBRATE ANOTHER YEAR OF GROWTH!

Saturday, September 22
DATE
6:30 p.m.
TIME
9 Briarfield Road
PLACE
Ellie O'Neill, 431-253-9007
R.S.V.P.

Steve is this old

Contents

The annual holiday triumvirate takes place in a mere six-week period, snowballing you at year's end. But entertaining during the high season doesn't have to be so harried. With these spirited ideas (think more fun, less formulaic), you'll find a warm, safe haven from that flurry of to-dos.

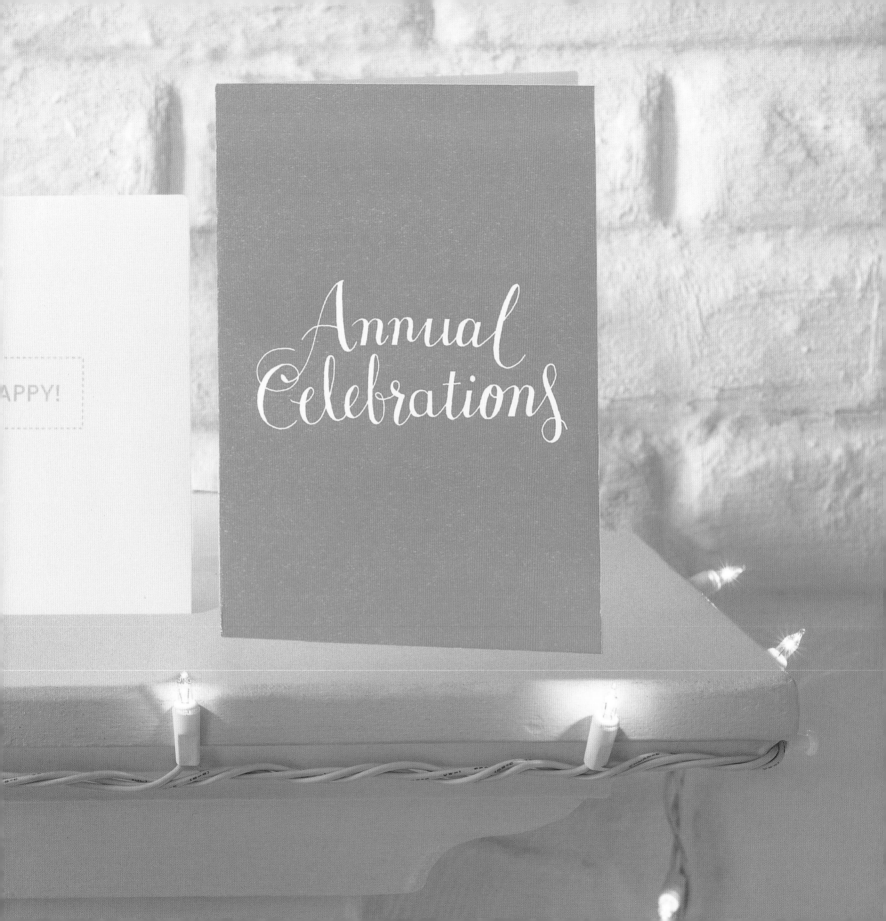

chapter 1 Thanksgiving Dinner

Some long-held traditions—counting your blessings, saying yes to that second slice of pie—deserve their place in the Thanksgiving repertoire. Others, like slaving over a homemade stuffing recipe (and never quite getting it right), do not. Especially when there's an easier and better alternative. This November, try a few time-saving twists on the traditions you don't necessarily treasure. Because too much fussing is for the birds.

Thanksgiving Dinner INVITATIONS

1. give them a hand

The hand-shaped construction-paper turkey is a Thanksgiving classic, so why not use it to extend a classic welcome to your guests? Have little ones trace a batch of turkeys, then cut out the birds and glue them to note cards. Draw in the wattle and whatnot, and write the dinner details inside.

2. special thanks

Repurpose thank-you cards as invitations. They don't all need to match (leftovers from several packs will work just fine), but they do need to say THANKS (not THANK YOU). Write "It's time to give…" above THANKS, and record the who, where, and when inside the card.

3. print-and-mail template

This magnolia-leaf design is autumnal without being a bit clichéd—and if you choose to use the magnolia-leaf decorating ideas in this chapter, the invitation gives guests a sneak preview of what's to come. To download and print this invitation template, go to www.realsimple.com/celebrations. Then use a hole punch to make a pair of holes near the "stem," thread in a ribbon, and tie a knot.

when to send

If all your guests live nearby, four weeks is enough notice for a Turkey Day invitation. But if some invitees will have to travel from far away, send theirs three to four months in advance.

Dear Farrow Family

PLEASE JOIN US FOR
THANKSGIVING DINNER

The Bowens'

WHERE

4:30 p.m.

WHEN

Your famous apple pie

with Cheddar cheese crust!

PLEASE BRING

(721) 274-2601

R.S.V.P.

1. self-serve station

If you're planning on having guests help themselves to the food, pull out the following tableware to place on a sideboard: a large, grooved-edge cutting board for the turkey (you can do the carving at the dinner table then transfer the whole thing to the buffet); bowls for the mashed potatoes and other vegetables; ovenproof casseroles for stuffing and sweet potatoes; and an elevated cake stand for the pie. Put the gravy boat on the dinner table.

2. lay it all out

Fumbling is OK in a touch-football game, but it's a big time-waster in your Thanksgiving kitchen. Before measuring that first half cup of flour, gather all the cooking tools you're going to need and line them up within arm's reach. Don't forget a couple of pot holders and a meat thermometer.

3. pressing matters

Consider splurging and send your formal table linens to the dry cleaners about a week in advance to have them cleaned and pressed. You may not have used them since last year's feast, and a year spent on a shelf can make linens a little musty.

4. go green

Leave the Indian corn in the attic. Magnolia leaves (sold at most florist shops) are a stylish, more surprising way to decorate your home. Start at the front door by tying a ribbon around a small bunch of branches and hanging them at eye level.

1. have seconds

To spare guests from having to say, "Please pass the [fill in the blank]," think in pairs when you set the table: Stock each end with its own water pitcher, bread basket, and bottles of red and white wine.

2. everyone in their place

For some families (you know who you are), assigned seating is as essential as the turkey at the Thanksgiving table. These magnolia-leaf place cards will guarantee maximum harmony. Tie a couple of leaves together with a ribbon, then write a guest's name on the top leaf with a gold-ink pen (sold at craft stores).

3. the good seats

Considering how long guests will be sitting on this feast-till-you-drop day, those folding chairs you use to round out the seating ought to be as comfortable as possible. Look for styles with wide back panels, sculpted (not flat) seats, and sturdy construction (sit in one to test it).

4. natural light

Use more magnolia leaves to create a series of glowing centerpieces. Drop large white pillar candles into clear, straight glass vases, then nest leaves around the candles. (Note: Be sure to keep the leaves safely away from the flame, and don't forget to check the leaves occasionally as the candles burn down.)

Thanksgiving Dinner FOOD & DRINK

With foolproof takes on traditional recipes—and a few savvy shortcuts—
you can pull off the annual juggling act with (relative) ease.

can't-go-wrong roast turkey

hands-on time: 15 minutes · total time: 3 hours,
30 minutes (includes resting)

- 1 10- to 12-pound turkey
- 3 tablespoons olive oil
- 1 tablespoon kosher salt
- 3/4 teaspoon black pepper

Heat oven to 425° F. Remove the turkey giblets. Rinse the turkey inside and out under cool running water, then pat dry with paper towels. Place the turkey on a wire rack in a metal roasting pan. Spread the oil evenly over the turkey and season with the salt and pepper. Roast the turkey until golden brown, about 45 minutes. Add about 1 cup of water to the pan and cover the turkey loosely with a large sheet of foil. Reduce heat to 375° F. Continue to roast until a thermometer inserted in a thigh registers 180° F, about 1 3/4 hours more, depending on the size of the turkey. Leave the foil in place and let the turkey rest for at least 30 minutes before carving. (If making gravy, reserve the pan drippings.)

can't-go-wrong gravy

hands-on time: 15 minutes · total time: 15 minutes

- 1 1/2 to 2 cups pan drippings from the turkey
- 2 tablespoons unsalted butter
- 4 tablespoons all-purpose flour
- 1/2 to 3/4 cup low-sodium chicken broth

Using a spoon, remove and discard the fat from the surface of the pan drippings. In a skillet, over low heat, melt the butter. Stirring constantly, sprinkle the flour over the butter. Cook, still stirring, until the mixture becomes a smooth paste, about 3 minutes. Still stirring constantly, slowly add the pan drippings, 1/2 cup at a time, and wait until the mixture is smooth before adding more. Add 1/2 cup of the broth and stir until smooth. For a thinner consistency, add more broth, a few tablespoons at a time.

classic mashed potatoes

hands-on time: 15 minutes • total time: 45 minutes

    4 pounds Yukon gold potatoes, peeled
      and quartered
$1/2$ cup heavy cream
    1 cup whole milk
    5 tablespoons unsalted butter
$2 1/4$ teaspoons kosher salt
$1/4$ teaspoon black pepper (optional)

Place the potatoes in a large pot. Add enough cold water to cover. Bring to a boil. Reduce heat and simmer until tender, about 15 minutes. Meanwhile, warm the cream and milk in a small saucepan over low heat. Drain the potatoes, return to pot, and mash. Stir in the warmed cream and milk, the butter, salt, and pepper (if using). (You can keep the potatoes warm in their serving bowl for up to 2 hours by placing the bowl over a pot of simmering water, covering the potatoes partially, and stirring occasionally. Just before serving, add a little extra milk and butter to achieve the original consistency.)

stuffing stir-ins

Sure, it's a bit sneaky, but it also saves precious time. Make two boxes of store-bought stuffing, then stir in one of the following fresh flavors before serving:

• $1 1/2$ cups chopped dried fruit (such as apricots, cherries, or golden raisins) and $1/2$ cup toasted chopped almonds or pecans.

• 4 sausage links and 1 diced apple. (Crumble the sausage and cook in a skillet for 1 minute. Add the apple and cook until the sausage is browned, 3 to 5 minutes.)
• 2 cups jarred chestnuts, crumbled, and 1 small red onion, diced and cooked in 2 tablespoons unsalted butter for 7 minutes.
• $1/2$ cup fresh herbs (such as sage, thyme, or parsley), roughly chopped, and a few spoonfuls of turkey drippings (fat skimmed off).

glazed sweet potatoes

hands-on time: 10 minutes • total time: 1 hour

    3 pounds sweet potatoes, peeled and
      sliced $1/4$ inch thick
$1/3$ cup light brown sugar
    3 tablespoons unsalted butter, cut into
      small pieces
    6 sprigs fresh thyme
$1 1/2$ teaspoons kosher salt
$1/4$ teaspoon black pepper

Heat oven to 425° F. Place the sweet potatoes in a 9-by-13-inch baking dish. Sprinkle with the sugar, butter, thyme, salt, and pepper. Cover tightly with foil. Bake until tender, about 30 minutes. Uncover, stir, and return to oven for 5 more minutes. Transfer to a serving dish.

what to do when

3 DAYS BEFORE
• Buy your turkey if you haven't already. Allow $3/4$ to 1 pound per person if you want just enough to make it through the meal, or $1 1/2$ pounds per person if you want leftovers for the long weekend.
• If using a frozen turkey, move it to the refrigerator to thaw.

2 DAYS BEFORE
• Make the cranberry sauce.

1 DAY BEFORE
• Read through each of the recipes to make sure you haven't forgotten any of the ingredients from the store.
• Bake the pie.

(timeline continued on following page)

what to do when

(continued)

THANKSGIVING MORNING
• If the turkey isn't fully defrosted, submerge it in cool water, changing the water every 30 minutes, until thawed.
• Prepare the stuffing stir-ins; set aside.
• Peel and slice the sweet potatoes. Toss with the remaining ingredients; set aside.

WHILE THE TURKEY ROASTS
• Place the sweet potatoes on a second oven rack beneath the roasting pan and bake.
• Gather the ingredients for the gravy and the green beans.
• Make the mashed potatoes and keep them warm (see recipe for how to do this).

WHILE THE TURKEY RESTS
• Make the gravy and the green beans.

green beans with spiced nuts

hands-on time: 10 minutes • total time: 20 minutes

  2 pounds green beans
  2 tablespoons extra-virgin olive oil
  1/2 teaspoon kosher salt
  1/4 teaspoon black pepper
  1/2 cup store-bought spiced nuts, roughly chopped

Bring a large pot of salted water to a boil. Add the green beans and cook until almost tender, 3 to 5 minutes. Drain and transfer to a serving bowl. Add the oil, salt, pepper, and nuts and toss.

quick cranberry sauce

hands-on time: 15 minutes • total time: 2 hours, 45 minutes (includes cooling)

  4 cups (16 ounces) fresh or frozen cranberries
  1 1/2 cups (about 1 1/2 12-ounce jars) apple jelly or orange marmalade
  1/3 to 1/2 cup granulated sugar
  1/4 teaspoon grated orange zest (optional)

In a medium saucepan, over medium-high heat, combine the cranberries, jelly or marmalade, 1/4 cup water, sugar (1/3 cup if using jelly, 1/2 cup if using marmalade), and zest (if using). Bring to a boil. Reduce heat and simmer, stirring occasionally, until the cranberries burst and the sauce thickens, 7 to 10 minutes. (The mar-malade version will stay a bit runny.) Remove from heat; let cool. Transfer to a dish, cover, and refrigerate for at least 2 hours and up to 2 days.

caramel pecan pie

hands-on time: 10 minutes • total time: 3 hours, 20 minutes (includes cooling)

  1 1/4 cups (about 1 1/4 12-ounce jars) caramel sauce
  3 large eggs
  3 tablespoons unsalted butter, melted and cooled
  1/4 teaspoon kosher salt
  1 teaspoon vanilla extract
  2 cups (8 ounces) pecan halves
  1 refrigerated piecrust
     Whipped cream (optional)

Adjust an oven rack to the bottom position and heat oven to 325° F. In a bowl, whisk together the caramel sauce and eggs. Whisk in the butter, salt, and vanilla. Stir in the pecans. Fit the piecrust in a pie plate and place on a foil-lined baking sheet. Pour in the pecan mixture. Bake until center is set, 60 to 70 minutes. Transfer to a wire rack. Let cool for at least 2 hours. (You can refrigerate the pie for up to 2 days.) Serve with the whipped cream (if using).

what to sip

Serve both a red wine and a white, and let guests pick. Two to try: Zinfandel and Gewürztraminer.

Sometimes the people you're closest to are the ones you know the least about. So pose these questions to the table—the answers may surprise you.

childhood

- What was the home and the neighborhood you grew up in like?
- Which of your parents were you closer to?
- What was your role in your family?
- What were your siblings like back then, and how did you get along with them?
- What kind of student were you?
- Other than family, who were the most important people in your life?
- What were the happiest times of your childhood?
- What were the biggest disappointments?
- What were your hobbies?
- Who was the first person you ever kissed?
- What did you imagine your adult life would be like?

love and family

- Were you and your spouse in love from the start, or did it take time?
- What has been the most rewarding part about raising kids?
- What has been the most difficult part about raising kids?
- Do you have any good parenting advice?
- How are you like your parents? And how are you different?

work

- What was the best job you ever had? The worst?
- How did you decide what field to enter?
- Was there one person who had a big impact on your working life?
- If you had to do it all over again, would you choose the same career path?

likes and dislikes

- Who makes you laugh the hardest?
- Do you have a favorite book or author?
- Do you have a favorite movie?
- What was the best trip you ever took?
- If you could go somewhere you've never been, where would you go?
- If you could live anyplace in the world, where would it be?
- What are five things you couldn't live without?
- What's your most beloved personal possession?
- What's the bravest thing you've ever done?
- What's the scariest thing you've ever done? The dumbest?
- Is there anything you always wanted to do but never did?

life in general

- What were the best years of your life?
- What was the hardest decision you've made?
- What are the most important things in life?
- What do you consider to be your strongest character traits?
- What traits or habits do you wish you didn't have?
- Do you believe that people can change?
- Do you believe in God?
- Has life made you more hopeful or more cynical?
- What do you consider to be the biggest world events of your lifetime?
- Do you think life now is harder or easier than when you were young?
- What are you most proud of in your life?
- What do you hope to be remembered for?

Thanksgiving Dinner ETIQUETTE

It's inevitable: At least a few of these classic personality types will break bread at your Thanksgiving table. Here's how to manage them all.

the "constructive" criticizer

She offers advice on everything from your cranberry sauce to your spouse, but you didn't ask. You don't have to take the bait. Thank her for her suggestions, remind her that you have your reasons for the decisions you have made (you needn't spell them out), and move on. If she keeps offering her thoughts, try changing the subject or, in a pinch, cut her off with a friendly "Don't worry about me—I'm fine!"

the slacker

Sure, it would be nice if he set the table, washed a few dishes, or lit the candles on his own, but getting him to pitch in is probably as simple as asking. He truly may not realize that his help is needed, or he may assume that others can do a much better job. Give him a specific task with a few precise instructions and employ flattery if necessary. ("You have such an artistic eye. Would you mind arranging the raw veggies nicely on a platter?")

the control freak

Just as it's her prerogative to wear a sweater with turkeys and pilgrims, it's your right as host to celebrate the holidays in whatever way you like. Meaning you don't need to let her pressure you into saying grace, say, if you weren't planning on it. But there's room for both of you at the table—though you might want to sit at opposite ends for the sake of preserving your individual holiday spirits.

the exaggerator

People who chronically oversell their achievements, their children's achievements, heck, even their pets' achievements, often do so because they feel they have something to prove. Poking holes in an exaggerator's stories will only get him up in arms and possibly lead to even more outlandish claims. It's best to take the fish tales with a grain of (sea) salt.

the oversharer

If there's someone at the table who passes around gory details—medical, emotional, whatever—like they're dinner rolls, change the subject quickly every time he does it and eventually he'll get the message.

the whiner

For the family member who constantly feels he got the short end of the wishbone and wants to make sure everyone knows it: Ignore, ignore, ignore. Continue being polite and friendly, of course. Change the topic gracefully whenever possible, and refuse to let his bad mood, which is probably a ploy for attention, get you down.

the bully

Bullies often use mockery as a stunted way of connecting with others. And while old habits (like those dating back to playground days) are hard to break, it's never too late to start standing up for yourself. If he persists, turn away and exercise your right not to say anything to him at all. Or make light of his hectoring by countering with "And you obviously got the charm."

the busybody

By asking you every year, without fail, when you are going to get a man, get married, get pregnant, get a promotion, the busybody aims to make herself feel superior. You could try a shocking comeback to head the conversation into more amusing waters. For example: "I'm quitting my job, Aunt Jane, and moving to a commune. Didn't Mom tell you?" Or just politely ask why she is asking—and smile while you do it. This shifts the attention from your answers (or lack thereof) to the nosiness of the question, which often embarrasses the questioner enough to make her drop it.

the pontificator

Every family has one—the aunt, the cousin, or the grandfather who dominates every conversation. The best tactic for dealing with this motormouth: Seat him near those who are least likely to notice—the children. If the kids are at a separate table (and you don't think you can get away with putting him there, too), try to steer the dinner conversation away from topics he can't get enough of and toward ones in which somebody else is expert.

toast from the host

On Thanksgiving, why not open the toast up to everyone? After the turkey is carved and right before people start eating, raise your glass and express a few words of gratitude for those seated at the table. Then name one thing you're particularly thankful for this year, and allow the others to do the same.

Thanksgiving Dinner WRAP-UP

If you've done Thanksgiving right, you have leftovers. These tips will help you pack, store, and reinvent the remnants of the year's biggest meal.

roast turkey

HOW TO STORE IT: Rather than store the bird on a space-hogging platter, place the uncarved portion of the turkey in a disposable aluminum roasting pan (first remove any stuffing). Fold the pan up and around the turkey, molding the pan to conform to the bird's shape, cover with foil, and store on the bottom shelf of the refrigerator.

HOW LONG IT LASTS: 3 to 4 days. (You can remove the turkey meat from the bones and freeze for up to 3 months.)

HOW TO USE IT: Make a quesadilla by layering turkey, mashed potatoes, cranberry sauce, and mozzarella or Monterey Jack cheese between tortillas; then heat. You can also use turkey in any recipes that call for leftover chicken.

gravy

HOW TO STORE IT: In a shallow, airtight container in the refrigerator.

HOW LONG IT LASTS: 1 to 2 days.

HOW TO USE IT: Spoon it over biscuits for breakfast. Or pour it over baked potato wedges (the kind you keep in the freezer) for a diner favorite known as "wet fries."

cranberry sauce

HOW TO STORE IT: In an airtight container in the refrigerator. (Never leave canned cranberry sauce in an open can—the metal can leach into the sauce.)

HOW LONG IT LASTS: 3 to 4 days.

HOW TO USE IT: Warm the sauce and spoon it over vanilla ice cream, or make a peanut butter–and-cranberry sandwich.

green beans

HOW TO STORE THEM: In an airtight container in the refrigerator.

HOW LONG THEY LAST: 3 to 4 days.

HOW TO USE THEM: Stir-fry them with teriyaki sauce, leftover turkey, and water chestnuts or some other vegetables.

mashed potatoes

HOW TO STORE THEM: In an airtight container in the refrigerator.

HOW LONG THEY LAST: 3 to 4 days. (You can freeze the rest for up to 3 months.)

HOW TO USE THEM: Create a mashed potato omelet (spoon potatoes over a partially set egg in a skillet, then fold the egg over). Or make potato pancakes: Add a beaten egg to cold mashed potatoes, form into patties, and fry in butter or olive oil.

sweet potatoes

HOW TO STORE THEM: In an airtight container in the refrigerator.

HOW LONG THEY LAST: 3 to 4 days.

HOW TO USE THEM: Mash the leftover sweet potatoes into a puree and drizzle with maple syrup. Or add additional vegetable or chicken broth to the puree to create a soup and garnish with a few shelled pumpkin seeds.

stuffing

HOW TO STORE IT: In an airtight container in the refrigerator.

HOW LONG IT LASTS: 3 to 4 days.

HOW TO USE IT: Make a casserole. Place shredded leftover turkey in a buttered baking dish, drizzle with gravy, and top with stuffing. Bake in a 350° F oven until warmed through. Cut into squares.

chapter 2 *Holiday Open House*

Ah, December! There's no month of the year when you have more of a desire to entertain—and less time to actually do it. This holiday season, instead of attempting a dressed-up event, like dinner or cocktails, take an easier tack. A casual, come-and-go family open house keeps the focus on the people, not the preparation, and allows you to make merry with *all* your loved ones—including those who still believe in Santa Claus.

Holiday Open House INVITATIONS

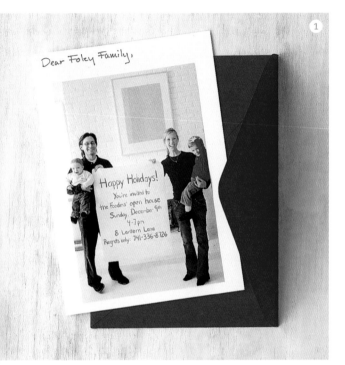

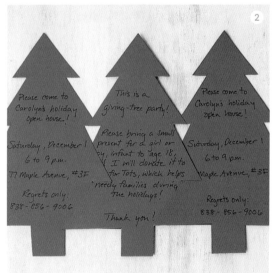

1. get the picture

How's this for a December time-saver? Combine your holiday card with your open-house invitation. Take a photo of your family holding a large sheet of paper that wishes people a happy holiday and also lists the party's specifics. Mount the photo on card stock.

2. presents required

Make your party a giving-tree party. Ask each guest to bring a present for a needy child, then donate the gifts to a local charity. Be as specific as possible: the charity you're donating to, the age ranges of the children to buy for, a ballpark figure for what to spend, etc.

3. print-and-mail template

A miniature candy cane, a jingle bell, or a slim ornament can turn a simple invitation into a sweet gift. Download and print out the invitation at www.realsimple.com/celebrations. Then punch a hole in the top of the card, loop a ribbon through, attach your chosen seasonal touch, and mail the whole thing in a padded envelope.

when to send

Most people's calendars fill up quickly at this time of year, so mail your invitations about a month in advance to make sure there's room for your party in your invitees' busy schedules.

CELEBRATE

The Kellers

INVITE

The Hycles

TO A HOLIDAY OPEN HOUSE ON

Saturday, December 15th
4 to 8 p.m.

AT

673 Park Terrace

R.S.V.P. BEFORE December 11th

BY PHONE (488) 214-1552

BY E-MAIL theKellers@myemail.com

CELEBRATE

The Kellers

INVITE

The Parks

TO A HOLIDAY OPEN HOUSE ON

Saturday, December 15th
4 to 8 p.m.

AT

673 Park Terrace

R.S.V.P. BEFORE December 11th

BY PHONE (488) 214-1552

BY E-MAIL theKellers@myemail.com

1. warmer welcome

Wave good-bye to the same old wreath and hello to guests arriving at your front door. Buy a pair of children's mittens—or just gather up two orphans from your own pile—and dangle them from a wreath with ribbon. (A thin wire threaded through the wrists of the mittens will give the ribbon a loop to pass through.)

2. coat room

Rent or buy a clothing rack for guests to hang their coats on as they arrive. If you suspect there will be an abundance of look-alike black wool styles, you may want to provide stick-on name tags so guests can label theirs and avoid post-party mix-ups.

3. mantel pieces

Want a refreshing treatment for a mantel or a ledge? Scatter clementines and peppermint balls along an evergreen swag. The end result will look so inviting, nibblers may just pick it clean by the party's end.

4. white Christmas

A lesson learned from Charlie Brown's lovably feeble tree: Spare can be beautiful. Trim a small, artificial white tree with objects that share a similar color scheme—say, candy canes, peppermints, and red-orange bows—and place it on a side table or a coffee table.

3. fashion plate

Wrap each dish in a sheet of parchment paper and tie with a length of ribbon before stacking on the buffet. Guests will be rewarded with a pretty presentation (not to mention a little gift-opening practice).

1. the great cover-up

A white linen tablecloth is fine for fancy dinners but can seem a tad stiff for a casual get-together. Instead, warm up a buffet with a richly colored wool camping blanket.

2. mismatched napkins

Using an eclectic collection of dish towels as napkins saves you the trouble of pressing your linens before the party—and cursing red lipstick afterward. One caveat: Don't include faded, frayed older towels in the mix. Those should stick to dish drying.

4. five-second centerpiece

Mound a mix of clementines and peppermint balls in a single glass compote (or a grouping of three). At the end of the night, have the kids portion the contents into cellophane goody bags for guests to take home.

Holiday Open House FOOD & DRINK

Prepare these dishes ahead of time and they'll sit happily for hours. Because you shouldn't be cooking during the party—you should be at the brownie bar.

menu

ALL RECIPES SERVE 6 TO 8

rosemary olives

store-bought spiced nuts

cured meats

bakery bread

smoked salmon with crème fraîche

baked risotto torte

frisée, bacon, and dried cranberry salad

brownie bar

pomegranate punch

rosemary olives

hands-on time: 5 minutes • total time: 10 minutes

    1 pint (2 cups) mixed olives
  1/4 cup olive oil
    3 sprigs fresh rosemary, leaves picked

In a saucepan, over low heat, combine the olives, oil, and rosemary leaves. Warm until heated through, about 7 minutes. Serve warm or at room temperature, alongside a bowl of store-bought spiced nuts. (You can make the olives early in the day and leave them at room temperature for up to several hours.)

cured meats

hands-on time: 5 minutes • total time: 5 minutes

1 1/2 pounds cured meats, including salami, prosciutto, and bresaola

Arrange the meats on a cutting board. (You can cover and refrigerate the cured meats for up to several hours before serving.) If you are not using precut meats, thinly slice a few pieces, then leave the knife on the board so guests can slice the rest. Serve with bakery bread.

smoked salmon with crème fraîche

hands-on time: 10 minutes • total time: 10 minutes

  3/4 cup crème fraîche or sour cream
  1/2 pound sliced smoked salmon
    2 tablespoons chopped fresh dill
    1 lemon, cut into wedges
       Toast points (optional)

Place the crème fraîche or sour cream in a small serving bowl. Arrange the salmon on a platter, separating the individual slices, and sprinkle with the dill. (You can cover and refrigerate the crème fraîche and salmon separately for up to 24 hours.) Serve the lemon wedges and toast points (if using) on the side.

baked risotto torte

hands-on time: 35 minutes • total time: 2 hours

> 3 cups low-sodium chicken broth
> 3 tablespoons olive oil, plus more
>   for the pan
> 1 medium yellow onion, finely chopped
> 4 cloves garlic, finely chopped
> 1¹/4 cups Arborio rice
> ¹/2 cup dry white wine
> ¹/4 teaspoon kosher salt
> ¹/4 teaspoon black pepper
> 1¹/4 cups (5 ounces) grated Parmesan
> 3 tablespoons chopped fresh flat-leaf parsley

Heat oven to 400° F. Warm the broth in a small saucepan over low heat. Meanwhile, heat the oil in a large saucepan over medium heat. Add the onion and cook for 5 minutes. Add the garlic and cook for 2 minutes. Add the rice and cook, stirring constantly, until it begins to turn translucent, about 1 minute. Add the wine and cook, stirring often, until the liquid is absorbed, 3 to 5 minutes. Ladle ¹/2 cup of the broth into the rice mixture and cook, stirring occasionally, until the liquid is absorbed. Repeat with the remaining broth, ¹/2 cup at a time, until the rice is tender but still slightly firm, about 25 minutes total. Stir in the salt, pepper, and ¹/2 cup of the Parmesan. Remove from heat. Cool for 5 minutes.

Meanwhile, oil a 9-inch springform pan, large ovenproof skillet, or 9-inch cake or pie pan.

Sprinkle ¹/4 cup of the Parmesan in the pan. Pour in the risotto. (You can cover and refrigerate for up to 1 day.) Sprinkle ¹/4 cup of the remaining Parmesan over the top. Bake for 30 minutes. Let cool in pan for 30 minutes. If using a springform pan, remove ring; if using a skillet or other pan, leave the risotto torte in pan. In a bowl, combine the remaining Parmesan with the parsley. Sprinkle over the top of the torte. Slice into wedges. Serve warm or at room temperature.

frisée, bacon, and dried cranberry salad

hands-on time: 20 minutes • total time: 20 minutes

> 4 ounces (about 5 slices) bacon,
>   cut into ¹/2-inch pieces
> 3 tablespoons extra-virgin olive oil
> 1¹/2 teaspoons Dijon mustard
> 1¹/2 teaspoons fresh lemon juice
> ¹/2 teaspoon granulated sugar
> ¹/8 teaspoon kosher salt
> ¹/8 teaspoon black pepper
> 2 large heads (about ³/4 pound total)
>   frisée, torn into pieces
> 3 tablespoons dried cranberries

Fry the bacon in a skillet over medium heat. Transfer to paper towels. Meanwhile, in a large serving bowl, whisk together the oil, mustard, lemon juice, sugar, salt, and pepper. Add the frisée; toss. Top with the bacon and cranberries.

what to do when

1 DAY BEFORE

• Arrange the smoked salmon on a platter, put the crème fraîche in a bowl, and cover and refrigerate both.

• Assemble the cured meats on a cutting board, but don't slice anything. Cover and refrigerate.

• Assemble the risotto torte, but do not bake it. Cover and refrigerate.

EARLY IN THE DAY

• Warm the olives and set aside at room temperature.

• Bake the brownies.

• Assemble all the ingredients for the salad (except the bacon) and the brownie bar (except the whipped cream).

(timeline continued on following page)

what to do when

(continued)

**1 HOUR BEFORE
GUESTS ARRIVE**

• Bake the risotto torte,
let cool, and unmold.
• Fry the bacon and toss
the salad.
• Fill several bowls
with the store-bought
spiced nuts.
• Mix both punch recipes
in their serving bowls,
cover, and refrigerate—
but don't add the
ice until guests start
to arrive.

**JUST BEFORE
GUESTS ARRIVE**

• Whip the cream for
the brownies.
• Thinly slice a
few pieces from the
cured meats.
• Add ice to the bowls
of punch.

brownie bar

**hands-on time: 10 minutes • total time: 1 hour,
15 minutes (includes cooling)**

This DIY dessert spread is entirely store-bought, but that won't stop kids and adults alike from digging in (multiple times).

Start with a box of brownie mix. Pour the batter into a 9-inch springform or cake pan lined with an 11-inch circle of parchment paper. (This will create the pretty fluted edge shown opposite; use an overturned mixing bowl to trace a circle on the parchment.) Bake at 350° F for about 35 minutes; let cool. If using a springform pan, remove ring. If using a cake pan, invert onto a plate, then invert again. Place the brownie (still in the parchment) on a cake stand. Surround it with bowls of...

WHIPPED CREAM

Beat 1 pint of heavy cream with 3 tablespoons of confectioners' sugar until stiff peaks form. The cream should remain whipped for at least an hour. Keep watch and remove it from the table when the peaks start to sag. (Note: If you don't want to babysit the whipped cream during your open house, omit the cream and put several pints of vanilla ice cream on ice in a bucket or bowl instead.)

CHOCOLATE OR FUDGE SAUCE

Since the sauce plays such a big role in this dessert, it pays to splurge on a specialty label.

DULCE DE LECHE

This Latin-American delicacy, made by slowly simmering milk and sugar until the sugars caramelize, is rich, creamy, and fabulously sweet. It's available in cans or jars at many supermarkets.

pomegranate punch

hands-on time: 5 minutes • total time: 5 minutes

1 1/2 cups (12 ounces) vodka, chilled
  2 cups (16 ounces) cranberry juice
    cocktail, chilled
  2 cups (16 ounces) pomegranate
    juice, chilled
  3 tablespoons fresh lime juice

In a large punch bowl or pitcher, combine all the ingredients. (You can cover and refrigerate for up to several hours.) Add ice and ladle into plastic party cups or martini glasses.

To make a kids' version: Substitute 1 1/2 cups (12 ounces) chilled lemon-lime soda for the vodka. Place the punch on a separate serving table—far away from the spiked recipe—and label the bowl or pitcher FOR KIDS ONLY.

At an all-ages party, it pays to have something to keep the young—
and the young at heart—entertained and occupied.

snow job

When picking up decorating supplies, buy an extra box of clementines for kids to make these melt-proof snowmen. (An adult may need to supervise, depending on the kids' ages.)

- Give each child three clementines, a sturdy plate, some toothpicks, and store-bought frosting.
- Dollop frosting in the center of the plate and place a large clementine in it. Stick a few toothpicks halfway into the top of the fruit and spear a smaller clementine on top. Repeat with the third clementine.
- Make a hat out of frosting, a vanilla wafer, and peppermints. Use candy-cane pieces for arms and a nose, and cloves for the eyes. And tie on a scarf of red licorice.

chain gang

This is the perfect low-maintenance party project: no glue, no scissors, and no supervision necessary. Hand kids squares of aluminum foil (cut them ahead of time, or use precut deli-style sheets) and demonstrate how to mold them into links to make a chain. When the kids get home, they can show off their handiwork by stringing the chains on their Christmas trees.

spring ahead

Let guests make their own garden-starting goody bags. Place a tray with paperwhite-narcissus bulbs, squares of burlap, a roll of twine, and scissors near the front door. Put a note by the tray, inviting guests to wrap up three or four bulbs in the burlap to take home with them. And provide copies of the following instructions for forcing the bulbs to bloom early: "Fill a tall vase with stones and enough water to nearly reach the top of the stones without covering them. Drop in a bulb root-side down, making sure the bulb isn't touching the water. Refill the vase with water as needed. In a few weeks, the bulb will begin to send up leaves and, later, blooms."

ghosts of Christmas past

Treat your friends and family to a little holiday nostalgia. Project an old home movie of Christmas Day on the wall of your living room (to rent a projector, check your local Yellow Pages for audio-visual equipment), play a classic holiday film on the television (on mute), or buy a virtual-fireplace video (available at many novelty stores), featuring a solid two hours of burning logs. If partygoers tire of small talk, they can tune in to the on-screen ambience.

Holiday Open House ETIQUETTE

An open house should be a cozy affair, but not so cozy that manners don't matter. This advice will help you achieve peace at the party (if not on earth).

How do I encourage people to come within the designated open-house hours—and not five minutes before the party is supposed to end?

The way to a guest's punctuality, like the way to his heart, is often through his stomach. Specifying times for when food and drink will be served ("The buffet and punch will be ready at 4 P.M. sharp") will motivate guests to arrive before the cocktails run dry or the buffet is picked over. Another technique is to mark the party's ending time as an hour earlier than you'd like the place to clear out, so that you can enjoy the company of any latecomers without staring at your watch the whole time.

Is it OK to nudge someone who hasn't RSVP'd?

Including a respond-by date on the invitation is the first step toward making sure you get a timely head count, but if the date passes and you still haven't heard from someone, don't hesitate to pick up the phone. Before you even begin to ask, a bell may go off in her head, prompting her to inform you of her plans. In any case, failing to RSVP is a much worse offense on anyone's etiquette scale than reminding someone that she hasn't.

How can I stop my friend's first grader from bringing the house down fragile heirloom by fragile heirloom?

Disciplining other people's kids is a tricky proposition, so the best tactic is to try to avoid it in the first place. Bear in mind the three P's: prevention, preparation, and protectiveness.

• Prevention: Before the party starts, put any valuable breakables out of reach of little hands or in another room entirely, and close the doors to any rooms you don't want kids spending time in.

• Preparation: Along with the chain- and snow-man-making activities described on page 43, consider setting aside a play space and stocking it with games, toys, and other distractions to keep kids busy and out of trouble for the duration of the evening. (After all, it's when they get bored that they start using a clementine as a football.)

- Protectiveness: If a child's rambunctious behavior escalates so much that you need the parent to take action, frame your concern as one for the child's safety and not for your possessions: "Judy, I'm sorry to bother you, but I'm afraid James is going to crack his head open on my glass coffee table! Could you kindly intervene?"

What should I do if my child says something rude to a guest?

If little Johnny has just told Aunt Sally that she looks exactly like Santa Claus, your mortification may tempt you to give him a good scolding on the spot, but don't. Spontaneity and honesty are admirable qualities in children that should be reined in but not squashed. A better strategy is to redirect attention with a new topic or activity for Johnny to focus on away from Aunt Sally. Then give her a brief, lighthearted apology and even laugh the incident off a bit so she doesn't take it as a serious, intentional affront. Later, explain to Johnny that there are some things he shouldn't say out loud because they can be hurtful to another person.

Do I have to set out the dish one of my guests brought over, unasked?

Though you didn't request that guests contribute food, your neighbor Betty showed up with her famous tuna surprise. As much as it might pain you to place the casserole amid your carefully chosen spread, there is no polite way to avoid serving a dish that someone has brought to an open house or a potluck. All you can do is thank the kind cook and set the food on the table—no matter how badly that tuna clashes with the rest of the flavors. On the other hand, you *don't* have to serve the bottles of wine guests bring. They probably consider the wine a hostess gift, and you should have no qualms about saving it for another occasion.

toast from the host

An open-house toast may not be typical, but it's a great opportunity to wish everyone a happy holiday. Give yours about an hour after the party has started, and don't worry about making sure nearly every party guest is present, because if you wait too long, early-arriving guests may leave before you speak. The message should be kept short and sweet, especially if children are there. Try "Thank you so much for coming to our open house. Our home is warmer, happier, and merrier with all of you inside it."

Holiday Open House WRAP-UP

With a smart cleanup strategy and a savvy tactic to shoo out the last guests, your holiday spirit will stay intact.

during the party

Make sure the second wave of visitors isn't greeted by empty casseroles and piles of crumpled napkins—and that you aren't greeted by an overwhelming mess when everyone takes off.

- Set out multiple trash baskets for guests to deposit refuse in. Plant one near the buffet, another near the punch, and one at the activities table. Change all trash bags halfway through the evening, if necessary.
- Every hour or so, make a quick sweep of the party, collecting used items and tossing them in the sink or the garbage. Refresh the buffet as needed.
- Or...forget these strategies entirely and hire a young relative or neighbor to do it all for you.

after the party

Here's what tasks to do after the guests leave— and what can wait until later.

WHAT TO DO THAT NIGHT

- Package and store any leftover food.
- Load as many dishes as possible into the washer so you'll have room to get pots and pans in and out of the sink and a place to set them for drying.
- Put the pots and pans in a sinkful of hot, soapy water to soak. Wash and dry the ones that can't sit in suds all night.
- Empty all trash cans containing food and drink remnants.
- Check carpets and furniture for spills, and spot-clean all stains with cold water and dish detergent.

WHAT TO DO THE NEXT DAY

- Wash and dry the pots that have been soaking.
- Wipe down countertops, the backsplash, and the area surrounding the stove with disinfectant.
- Use an electrostatic mop to pick up dirt and hair. (This will make it easier to do wet-mopping later.)
- Clean any bathrooms used by guests.

WHAT TO DO WHENEVER

- Mop and vacuum.
- Launder dish towels used as napkins and hand towels from the guest bathroom.

the signal to go

Want a gentle-yet-effective way to let guests know your open house is closing? When the time approaches, bring out a tray of treats that bear a subtle message: hot chocolate in paper party cups with the phrase THANKS FOR COMING! written on them. Add peppermint-stick stirrers to sweeten the deal.

chapter 3 New Year's Eve Potluck

A fresh year rife with possibility, a crowd of close friends, a great cocktail dress—what more reason do you need to celebrate on December 31? Here's one: This New Year's Eve party is a potluck. With most of the food-making duties off your shoulders (and onto those of your generous friends), you'll be able to send the old year off with a bang, without knocking yourself out. Here's to the happiest New Year yet.

New Year's Eve Potluck INVITATIONS

1. unfurl the fun

Use a party blower to announce your shindig. Just unroll the curl and paste on a message like "Come to our New Year's Eve blowout!" (You can put the party details on a separate card.) Mail in a padded envelope.

2. perfect timing

Start the New Year's countdown early with this homemade clock. Draw the face on a piece of card stock and attach hour and minute hands with a brass fastener. Then mark off the evening's most important moments: when guests should arrive, when the corks will start popping, and when you'd like to be tucked in bed.

3. print-and-mail template

Who wouldn't crack a smile at a Mad Libs invitation? But this card does more than entertain—it also makes party planning easier. Print out the template at www.realsimple.com/celebrations and fill in a dish for each guest to bring (enclose a recipe, if you wish). The bottom portion lets guests RSVP *and* make a song request, so you can put together a party playlist.

when to send

Because New Year's Eve is arguably the biggest party night of the year, tell guests you're planning on having people over well ahead of time. Then mail the actual invitations right after Thanksgiving.

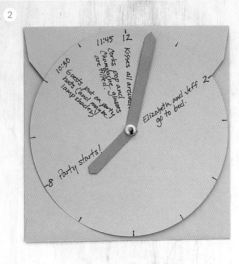

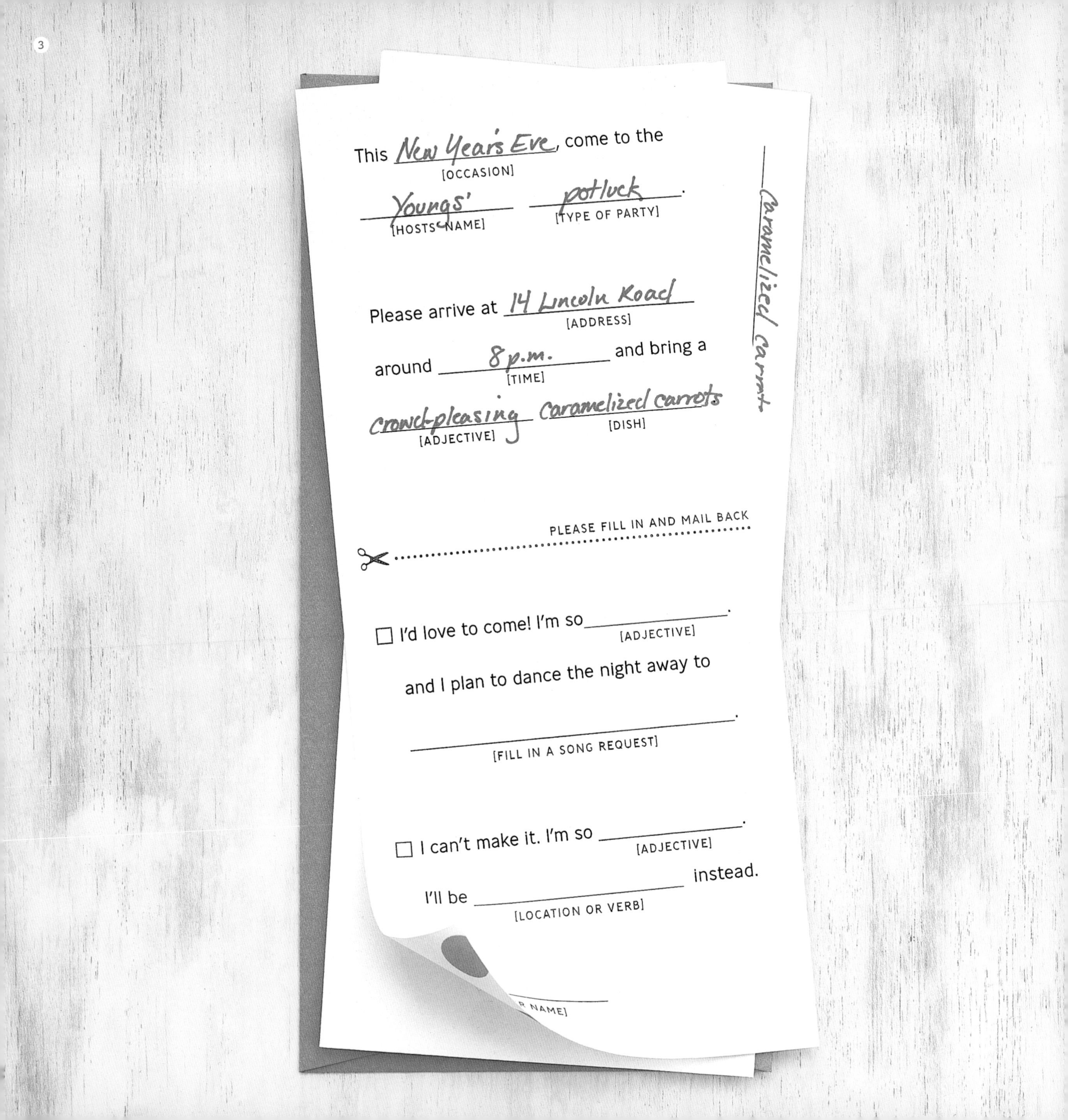

This *New Year's Eve*, come to the
[OCCASION]

_____*Youngs'*_____ _____*potluck*_____ .
[HOSTS' NAME]   [TYPE OF PARTY]

Please arrive at _____*14 Lincoln Road*_____
[ADDRESS]

around _____*8 p.m.*_____ and bring a
[TIME]

crowd-pleasing *Caramelized carrots*
[ADJECTIVE]   [DISH]

Caramelized carrots

· · · · · · · · · · · · · · · · · · · PLEASE FILL IN AND MAIL BACK

✂ ·

☐ I'd love to come! I'm so_____.
[ADJECTIVE]

and I plan to dance the night away to

_____ .

_____
[FILL IN A SONG REQUEST]

☐ I can't make it. I'm so _____.
[ADJECTIVE]

I'll be _____ instead.
[LOCATION OR VERB]

_____
[R NAME]

1. bright idea

Give those strands of holiday lights one more starring role before they head back to storage. When coiled in bottomless hurricane lamps, they make a glowing addition to a mantel or a sideboard. Run both the socket and plug ends of each strand out from underneath its cylinder, connect the cords to one another, and insert the last plug into a wall outlet.

2. dig in

For added touches of festivity, fill clear vases or bowls with silver- or gold-wrapped Hershey's Kisses, party blowers, and noisemakers (what's New Year's without a little noise?).

3. good favor

In the American South, black-eyed peas are served on New Year's Day in hopes that they'll bring a year filled with luck. Send guests home with small cellophane bags of peas—sealed with GOOD LUCK stickers—to cook up the next day. (If you wish, include the recipe for Black-Eyed Peas with Greens, page 59, in each bag.)

4. tie one on

Save pieces of ribbon left over from holiday gift wrapping to knot around the stems of your Champagne flutes. Bonus: Using a different color for every flute will help guests keep track of their glasses.

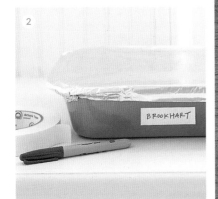

3. table labels

There's no need to spend the evening deconstructing the buffet ("And here we have the caramelized carrots"). Using a knife, make a slit in the ends of wine corks. Then slide a card into each slit to identify all the dishes.

1. pipe up

Pipe cleaners, those staples of elementary-school art class, are also a smart and surprising solution for holding napkins and utensils together. Twist a few metallic ones around each bundle and arrange the ends in a starburst.

4. time to reflect

Give your dining table a whole new image with a frameless full-length mirror. Laid flat down the center, it serves as a runner, reflecting everything—candles, glassware, confetti—that rests on top of it.

2. sign in, please

As guests arrive, provide them with masking tape and markers so they can label the bowls and the casserole dishes they've brought. That way, you won't be left with a cabinetful of unfamiliar cookware and no idea of what belongs to whom.

New Year's Eve Potluck FOOD & DRINK

Assign one of these easy-to-make potluck recipes to each of your party guests and watch the insta-dinner come together, as if by magic.

kir royales

hands-on time: 5 minutes • total time: 5 minutes

6 to 8 tablespoons crème de cassis
(black currant liqueur)

1 bottle Champagne, Prosecco, or some
other sparkling wine, chilled

6 to 8 raspberries (fresh or frozen
and thawed)

Pour 1 tablespoon of crème de cassis into each Champagne flute. Add enough sparkling wine to fill the glass 3/4 to the top. Drop 1 raspberry into each flute.

potato and onion flat bread

hands-on time: 15 minutes • total time: 35 minutes

2 tablespoons olive oil

1 small yellow onion, thinly sliced into circles

1 russet potato, peeled and thinly sliced

2 sprigs fresh rosemary, leaves picked

1 teaspoon kosher salt

1/4 teaspoon black pepper

1 tablespoon cornmeal for the skillet

1 package (about 1 pound) refrigerated
pizza dough

Heat oven to 450° F. Heat the oil in a large skillet over medium heat. Add the onion and cook until golden, 5 to 7 minutes. Remove from heat. Add the potato, rosemary leaves, salt, and pepper and toss; set aside. Sprinkle a baking sheet with the cornmeal. Place the dough on a work surface, shape into a 12-inch round, and transfer to the prepared sheet. Spoon the potato mixture over the dough, leaving a 1-inch border. Bake until golden, about 20 minutes. Slice into wedges. Serve warm or at room temperature.

roast chicken with lemon and thyme

hands-on time: 15 minutes • total time: 1 hour, 15 minutes

2 3 1/2- to 4-pound chickens,
cut into pieces

1 teaspoon kosher salt

1 teaspoon black pepper
Zest of 2 lemons, cut into thin strips

1/2 cup fresh lemon juice

1 cup white wine

1/4 cup olive oil

2 cups kalamata olives, pitted

1 small bunch fresh thyme

Heat oven to 425° F. Rinse the chicken and pat dry with paper towels. Place in a roasting pan. Season with 1/2 teaspoon of the salt and 1/2 teaspoon of the pepper. In a small bowl, combine the lemon zest and juice, wine, oil, and the remaining salt and pepper. Pour the mixture over the chicken. Scatter the olives and thyme sprigs over the top. (You can cover and refrigerate for up to 12 hours.) Roast until golden, about 20 minutes. Reduce heat to 375° F. Continue to roast until the chicken is cooked through, about 40 minutes more. Transfer the chicken (but not the juices) to a platter and spoon the olives over the top. Serve warm or at room temperature.

black-eyed peas with greens
hands-on time: 20 minutes • total time: 25 minutes

- 2 10-ounce boxes frozen black-eyed peas (thawed), or 2 15-ounce cans black-eyed peas (drained), or 8 ounces (about 1 1/4 cups) dried black-eyed peas
- 2 teaspoons olive oil
- 1/2 pound ham steak, cut into 1/2-inch dice
- 2 bunches Swiss chard, rinsed
- 1/2 teaspoon kosher salt
- 1/4 teaspoon black pepper
- 2 teaspoons balsamic vinegar

If using frozen peas, cook them according to the package directions, drain, and transfer to a large bowl. If using canned peas, drain and transfer to a large bowl. If using dried peas, place them in a large pot, add enough water to cover by 1 inch, simmer for about 20 minutes, drain, and transfer to a large bowl. Heat 1 teaspoon of the oil in a large pot over medium-high heat. Add the ham and cook until browned, about 3 minutes. Transfer to bowl. Meanwhile, separate the Swiss chard stems from the leaves and slice both crosswise into 1-inch-wide pieces. Heat the remaining oil in the pot over medium heat. Add the stems and cover. Cook until softened, about 3 minutes. Add the leaves, cover, and cook, stirring occasionally, until wilted, about 2 minutes. Add the Swiss chard, salt, pepper, and vinegar to the peas and ham and toss. Serve warm or at room temperature.

caramelized carrots
hands-on time: 15 minutes • total time: 35 minutes

- 1 tablespoon unsalted butter
- 1/2 cup plus 2 tablespoons olive oil
- 1/2 large yellow onion, finely chopped
- 1 teaspoon granulated sugar
- 1 teaspoon kosher salt
- 1 1/2 pounds carrots, peeled
- 1/2 cup sherry vinegar
- 1/4 teaspoon black pepper
- 1 teaspoon grated orange zest (optional)

Heat the butter and 2 tablespoons of the oil in a large skillet over medium heat. Add the onion, sugar, and 1/2 teaspoon of the salt and cook,

what to sip
If you prefer a full bar to count down to midnight, here's what to stock. Want to know how much to have on hand depending on the size of your party? Refer to *Real Simple* Party by Numbers, on the inside back cover.

ALCOHOL
Sparkling, white, and red wines. Beer, vodka, gin, rum, bourbon, whiskey, blended scotch, and dry vermouth.

MIXERS AND GARNISHES
Club soda or seltzer, tonic water, cola and diet cola, ginger ale, cranberry juice, orange juice, lemons, limes, and green olives (pitted).

TOOLS
Cocktail spoon, paring knife, cutting board, corkscrew, bottle opener, cocktail shaker, jigger or shot glass, and cocktail napkins.

New Year's Eve Potluck FOOD & DRINK

tip

Two days before the party, call or e-mail your guests to confirm they're bringing the dish you asked them to bring. If you don't want to make it sound like you're checking up on them (which, of course, you are), simply say you want to be sure to leave suitable space on the buffet for their delicious creations.

stirring occasionally, for 25 minutes. Meanwhile, bring a pot of water to a boil. Cut each carrot in half crosswise, then cut each half lengthwise into quarters. Add the carrots and 1/4 teaspoon of the remaining salt to the boiling water. Cook until tender, 4 to 6 minutes. Drain and pat dry. Transfer to a bowl, cover, and set aside. Add the vinegar to the cooked onions in the skillet. Cook for 1 minute. Add the pepper and the remaining oil and salt and stir. Remove from heat and cool for 5 minutes. Transfer the onion mixture to a blender and puree. Pour over the carrots and toss. Sprinkle with the zest (if using). Serve warm or at room temperature.

chocolate torte

hands-on time: 15 minutes • total time: 2 hours, 25 minutes (includes chilling)

- 1 stick unsalted butter
- 1/4 cup light corn syrup
- 8 ounces semisweet or dark chocolate, grated or finely chopped
- 1 large egg, lightly beaten
- 6 graham crackers or 8 biscuit cookies, broken into bite-size pieces
- 1/2 cup (2 ounces) chopped pecans
- 1/4 cup candied ginger or candied orange peel (optional)

Line a 9-inch round cake pan with a large sheet of aluminum foil, allowing a few inches to hang over the sides of the pan, or use an unlined 9-inch springform pan. Warm the butter and corn syrup in a large saucepan over low heat until the butter melts. Add the chocolate, remove from heat, and stir until smooth. Slowly stir in the beaten egg. Return to low heat, stirring, for 1 minute. Remove from heat; let cool. Add the crackers or cookies, half the pecans, and half the ginger or orange peel (if using) and combine. Transfer the mixture to the prepared pan. Top with the remaining pecans and ginger or orange peel (if using). Cover and refrigerate for at least 2 hours and up to 5 days. When ready to serve, use the foil as handles to transfer the entire cake to a platter, or if using a springform pan, remove ring and place the cake (and the bottom of the pan) on a platter. (Note: Because the egg in this recipe is not fully cooked, there is a risk of food-borne illness.)

late-night coffee

hands-on time: 5 minutes • total time: 5 minutes

- 6 cups strongly brewed black coffee
- 1/4 cup Kahlúa
- 3/4 cup Irish cream (such as Baileys)

In a large pitcher or bowl, combine the coffee, Kahlúa, and Irish cream. Pour into mugs. (Note: Be sure to brew a batch of straight coffee for the designated drivers.)

New Year's revelers typically arrive with those proverbial party hats on, but it never hurts to provide a few *literal* props and some memorable moments.

I see your future, and it is…

Fill a colorful gift bag or a box covered in festive paper with novelty items (sold at party-supply stores) and have guests reach in and grab an object to predict what kind of New Year they'll have. Examples: A toy airplane foretells travel; a (chocolate) gold coin, money; a paint set, new digs; a temporary tattoo, adventure; a ring, love; and a baby doll means start painting a nursery!

costume drama

Set a merrymaking mood by stocking a side table or a coatrack with Mardi Gras beads, boas, tiaras, top hats, funny sunglasses, and masks (all sold at party-supply stores). Provide one or two Polaroid instant cameras for guests to capture themselves in full regalia.

out with the old

Put the past year to rest in a tangible way by having guests write on small slips of colored paper one thing they'd like to forget about the previous 12 months (a bad fight, a bad habit, or even a bad haircut) and giving them scissors to cut the slips into tiny pieces. Scatter the confetti-like pieces along the mirrored table runner. Or, if you're not averse to vacuuming, collect all the scraps in a bowl and toss them into the air at midnight.

in with the new

Have each guest fill out a postcard with a New Year's resolution that will actually be a pleasure to keep (for example, "I will stop saying yes to every volunteer gig" or "I promise to get two massages next year"). And to make sure guests don't forget their resolutions, collect the post-cards and mail them to their authors a few months later as reminders.

The last hours of the year are full of what-to-do dilemmas—from opening a Champagne bottle like a pro to handling good guests gone bad.

How can I ask guests to bring a potluck item without feeling pushy?

Don't have a guilt trip about asking guests to contribute a dish—and telling them exactly what kind of dish, at that. People are usually happy to help out, and most prefer to be given guidance in these situations. Since you'll be specifying what dish to prepare on the invitation, make sure that your request is appropriate for the person. Consider who cooks every weekend and who orders takeout every night, as well as people's promptness. Your best friend is always on time and has delicious, stylish dishes down to a science? Ask her to bring the main course. Your cousin wouldn't know an oven mitt from a catcher's mitt and is sure to arrive 10 minutes before the ball drops? Suggest that she come with extra beverages.

Every year, I approach the Champagne bottle with trepidation. What's the best (and safest) way to pop the cork?

Thanks to this graceful (and, yes, injury-proof) technique, you'll never have to ask a friend to "do the honors" again.

• Make sure the bottle is thoroughly chilled, since a bottle at room temperature is at greater risk for foaming and spilling when opened.

• After you've removed the foil and the wire cage, hold the bottle's bottom in your right hand (or your left if you're a southpaw) and angle the bottle so it's pointing toward a corner of the ceiling.

• Grip the cork with your whole left fist (again, switch hands if you're a lefty), then twist the bottom of the bottle clockwise. Don't loosen your grip on the cork, twist the cork itself, or pull the cork away from the bottle. The slow twisting of the bottle will ease the cork out bit by bit. You'll know you've done it right when you hear a slight hissing sound, rather than a pop, as the cork comes out.

A guest has shattered my grand-mother's vase. What should I do?

Chances are, she feels deeply embarrassed and sorry, and showing your distress will only make both of you feel worse. So play down the mishap as graciously as you can, even if it means swallowing those tears. And get the mess out of the way as quickly as possible: Once the pieces are out of sight, it will be easier to push out of your mind and hers.

How do I deal with someone who is very tipsy (or full-on drunk)?

The first step, if you can do it, is to curtail his liquor consumption. If you're near the bar when he comes back for another drink, offer a glass of water instead and drink one yourself so as not to seem patronizing. This alone might send a message to him that he's had enough. If not, you may need to make arrangements for his ride home, either by calling a cab or asking another guest to drive him. Make sure you or someone else gets his keys if he resists being driven. And, finally, if the guest is nodding off on the sofa while the party carries on around him, enlist a couple of people to help you get him into a bed so that he can sleep it off.

What's the best way to let people know when it's time to shove off?

Send subtle, positive signals. Instead of launching into the plate-stacking, coat-retrieving, cleaning-up routine, tone down the mood by changing the music (say, from Madonna to Mozart). Then try handing out party favors while thanking people for coming. If the diehards still aren't getting it, offer "one last drink"—a nice way of being hospitable while making your point at the same time.

Can I send guests home with dirty casseroles instead of washing them all during the party?

Although you may feel awkward presenting guests with food-caked dishes, they would rather have your company than lose you to a pile of suds as they uncomfortably look on. If you still feel uneasy about it, say something like "I hope you don't mind being stuck with a dirty dish, but I don't want to hold everyone hostage while I wash up" as you make the handover.

toast from the host

A New Year's host should make her toast open to all partygoers, even tee-totalers, by providing an equally festive non-alcoholic alternative to Champagne (sparkling cider or mineral water splashed with fruit juice will do nicely). Then plan to make your toast about half an hour before the midnight countdown so that most guests will be settled in at the party, drinks in hand. Bear in mind that this is not the time for a lengthy monologue or an obscure quotation; stick to a heartfelt message of appreciation for their company and a wish for luck, health, peace, and prosperity.

New Year's Eve Potluck WRAP-UP

Auld acquaintances may be forgot in the New Year, but your party won't be if you send guests home with food—and a potentially profitable favor.

lucky numbers

Buy each guest a lottery ticket using digits from their telephone numbers or birthdays (or just use random digits, to make it easier on you) and hand out the tickets as guests depart. Keep your fingers crossed: If someone wins big, maybe she'll split the cash with you—or at least assume hosting duties for next year's celebration. (Dom Pérignon all around!)

take notes

Collect all the resolution-reminder postcards that guests wrote during the party, put a rubber band around the stack, and stash it in a safe place, like a desk drawer. Then mark a date on the calendar—say, late February or early March—to send them out. Bonus: Reading friends' resolutions before you mail them may give you a laugh—and a lift—during those dreary end-of-winter days.

keeping the bubbly bubbly

If you have any half-drunk bottles of sparkling wine left over, the best way to preserve their fizziness is to use a Champagne stopper (sold at cooking and wine stores) and store them in the refrigerator. They should remain drinkable for up to five days. As for those unopened bottles, store them on the bottom shelf of the refrigerator (where it's generally coldest). Luckily, most leftover hard liquor won't deteriorate like the sparkling stuff. Just cap the bottles tightly, keep them away from bright light, and they can last for years.

food for the road

Stock up on takeout containers, like Chinese-food cartons (sold at party-supply stores) or disposable resealable tubs (sold at supermarkets). Fill them with leftovers and send one home with each partygoer. Decorate the outside of each container with a label that reads, REHEAT, DRINK, AND BE MERRY.

No matter if you're saluting life, love, or simply a return to warm weather, the party you throw should be memorable *and* manageable. The following special events are surprisingly easy to stage. Now you'll have more time to toast the guest of honor—whether she's a new mom or Mother Nature.

11 MON	
12 TUE	
13 WED	
14 THU	
15 FRI	
16 SAT	Sarah's 30th Birthday — 6p.m.!
17 SUN	

Occasional Celebrations

chapter 4 # *A Shower*

When it comes to life's biggest events, you don't get much bigger than a wedding or the birth of a baby. And so it follows that the shower leading up to one of these occasions should be appropriately meaningful. Happily, this does not require slaving over a fantastically elaborate spread. To truly honor these new beginnings (and elicit *oohs* and *aahs* from your guests), all you need is a little creative vision and a few personal touches.

A *Shower* INVITATIONS

1. the perfect fit
Celebrating a truly well-matched couple? Send the wedding-shower invitation on a blank postcard-size puzzle (sold at paper-goods websites), using a heading like "Cara and Ethan: The Perfect Fit." Mail the puzzle unassembled so the recipient can put it together.

2. a novel idea
Make your baby-shower invitation into a mock library slip for the mom-to-be's "Great Expectations." Write the party details on a vertical index card, stamp the book's (er, baby's) due date at the bottom, and mail the card in a coin envelope. (Everything to make this invitation is sold at office-supply stores.)

3. print-and-mail template
This cheerful floral invitation is fitting for any kind of shower. Just download the invitation template from www. realsimple.com/celebrations, print it out, and fill in the pertinent details.

Mail wedding- and baby-shower invitations four to five weeks in advance to allow the guests plenty of time for gift buying. If a special guest is coming in from far away—say, a long-distance best friend or a mother-in-law—you may want to coordinate with her earlier to make sure she can be there on the date you've chosen.

you're invited to a *wedding* shower

FOR Mary Dwight

WHEN Sunday, May 19

WHERE Carrie's house

TIME 3 p.m.

RSVP before May 5

by phone 311-570-2185

by e-mail carrie@myemail.com

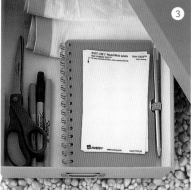

1. the simplest bouquet

Long considered mere filler (and un-wanted filler, at that), baby's breath is strikingly lovely on its own when gath-ered in a large, airy bunch. Sold at most florist shops, it's inexpensive and neutral enough to work in any setting. Drop a generous handful into a tall ceramic or glass vase.

2. alternative seating

If you don't have a dozen extra chairs lying around (or room to set them up if you do), provide throw pillows or ot-tomans for the (younger, more limber) guests to sit on. And, if possible, limit the gift-opening portion of the party to one hour or less. Any longer and *all* guests can start to get antsy.

3. gift-unwrapping stash

Stick the supplies the honoree will need under her chair so you won't have to part the sea of guests to fetch them in the middle of the party. In-clude scissors, large trash bags, a note-book and a pencil to record the gifts and their givers, and sticky labels to help keep similar gifts (such as plat-ters or glassware) straight.

4. take-home decorations

To give your shower a garden-party feel, buy small pots of thyme and slip in Popsicle sticks that identify the herb (and, thanks to a play on words, an-nounce the upcoming big day). Bonus: The plants double as party favors.

3. shake, rattle, and roll

For a baby shower, it's child's play to turn ho-hum white napkins into little bundles of joy. To make this sweet take on the napkin ring, knot a narrow ribbon around a plastic rattle, then loop the ribbon around the folded napkin and finish it off with a bow.

4. presents perfect

Instead of splurging on an elaborate (and probably expensive) centerpiece, let the guests' gifts do the work. Stack presents on the coffee or buffet table for an instant, eye-pleasing still life of patterned papers and pastel bows.

1. monogramming made easy

Block letter stamps turn a stack of blank matchboxes into custom favors. (You can find blank matchboxes and stamps at party-supply websites.) If you wish, make extra for the couple to use at their own parties. And try customizing some paper cocktail napkins, too (see page 83).

2. they go together

Garnish a wedding-shower table with Champagne glasses, each filled with a perfect coupling of jelly-bean flavors (coconut with pineapple, lemon with lime, cherry with vanilla)—edible proof that two together can be better than each alone.

A *Shower*, FOOD & DRINK

Each of these traditional shower delights—crustless tea sandwiches, dainty desserts, bubbly cocktails—comes with a little twist.

sweet pea soup

hands-on time: 10 minutes · total time: 20 minutes

- 4 tablespoons unsalted butter
- 2 cups finely chopped yellow onion
- 5 cups low-sodium chicken or vegetable broth
- 8 cups frozen green peas (from four 10-ounce packages), thawed slightly
- 1 1/2 cups loosely packed fresh mint leaves
- 2 teaspoons kosher salt
- 2 teaspoons granulated sugar

Melt the butter in a large saucepan over medium heat. Add the onion and cook until softened, 3 to 4 minutes. Add the broth, peas, mint, salt, and sugar. Remove from heat. Transfer half the mixture to a blender or food processor and puree until smooth. Repeat with the remaining soup. To serve the soup cold, transfer it to a bowl, cover, and refrigerate for at least 3 hours and up to 24 hours. To serve the soup hot, return it to pan and place over medium heat until warmed through. Ladle into teacups.

cucumber tea sandwiches

hands-on time: 10 minutes · total time: 10 minutes

- 2 English (seedless) cucumbers, ends trimmed
- 12 slices white sandwich bread
- 6 ounces whipped cream cheese
- 1 1/2 tablespoons finely chopped fresh dill

Cut each cucumber crosswise into 4 equal pieces. Thinly slice each cucumber piece lengthwise into strips. Place the bread slices on a work surface. Spread a thin layer of cream cheese onto each slice. Divide the cucumber and dill evenly among 6 of the slices (you may not need all the cucumber). Top with the remaining bread. Trim the crusts and cut into quarters.

chicken salad tea sandwiches

hands-on time: 20 minutes · total time: 20 minutes

- 1 3 1/2- to 4-pound rotisserie chicken, meat finely chopped
- 1/2 cup mayonnaise
- 1 teaspoon kosher salt
- 1/2 teaspoon black pepper
- 12 slices white sandwich bread

In a large bowl, combine the chicken, mayonnaise, salt, and pepper. Cover and refrigerate for at least 30 minutes and up to 2 days. Place 6 of the bread slices on a work surface. Divide the chicken salad evenly among the slices and top with the remaining bread. Trim the crusts and cut into quarters. (To upgrade this basic recipe, see New Takes on Chicken Salad, far right.)

egg salad tea sandwiches
hands-on time: 15 minutes · **total time: 15 minutes**

8 large eggs, hard-cooked and peeled
1/4 cup mayonnaise
1/4 teaspoon kosher salt
1/8 teaspoon black pepper
12 slices white sandwich bread

Grate the eggs using the large holes of a box grater. In a large bowl, combine the eggs, mayonnaise, salt, and pepper. Cover and refrigerate for at least 30 minutes and up to 5 hours. Place 6 of the bread slices on a work surface. Divide the egg salad evenly among the slices and top with the remaining bread. Trim the crusts and cut into quarters. (To upgrade this basic recipe, see New Takes on Egg Salad, far right.)

lemon squares
hands-on time: 25 minutes · **total time: 1 hour, 45 minutes (includes cooling)**

1 3/4 cups plus 3 tablespoons all-purpose flour
3/4 cup confectioners' sugar, plus more for sprinkling
1/2 teaspoon plus 1/8 teaspoon kosher salt
14 tablespoons (1 3/4 sticks) unsalted butter, chilled and cut into small pieces
4 large eggs
1 1/4 cups granulated sugar
1 tablespoon grated lemon zest
2/3 cup fresh lemon juice

Heat oven to 350° F. In a food processor, combine 1 3/4 cups of the flour, the confectioners' sugar, and 1/2 teaspoon of the salt. Pulse to blend. Add the butter and pulse until the mixture is crumbly. Knead the dough in the bowl until it comes together. Press the dough evenly into a 9-by-13-inch baking dish, pushing the dough up about 1/2 inch around the sides. Refrigerate for 15 minutes. Bake until golden brown, about 30 minutes. Meanwhile, in a large bowl, whisk together the eggs, granulated sugar, lemon zest, and the remaining flour and salt. Add the lemon juice and whisk until smooth. Pour the mixture over the hot crust. Reduce oven temperature to 300° F. Bake until the filling is set, about 15 minutes. Transfer dish to a wire rack and let cool. Dust with additional confectioners' sugar. Cut into 24 2-inch squares.

new takes on
CHICKEN SALAD

If desired, stir in one of the following to your recipe:

- 1 1/2 cups watercress and 1 Granny Smith apple, both finely chopped
- 1 pint quartered cherry tomatoes and 1/2 red onion, finely chopped
- 1 teaspoon curry powder and 1/2 cup jarred mango chutney
- 1/2 cup store-bought pesto

EGG SALAD

If desired, stir in one of the following to your recipe:

- 1 tablespoon chopped capers and 2 tablespoons chopped fresh flat-leaf parsley
- 1 tablespoon olive tapenade
- 1 teaspoon paprika and 1 tablespoon chopped fresh tarragon
- 1 tablespoon sweet relish

tip

When you serve the chocolate tea sandwiches, urge guests to eat them right away, before the chocolate starts to melt.

frozen chocolate tea sandwiches

hands-on time: 20 minutes • total time: 3 hours, 40 minutes (includes chilling)

3/4	cup whole milk
24	large marshmallows
12	ounces semisweet chocolate, grated or chopped
1 1/2	cups heavy cream
48	sugar cookies or 24 graham crackers

Line a 9-by-13-inch baking dish with foil, allowing the foil to hang over the sides. Heat the milk and marshmallows in a large saucepan over low heat, stirring often, until smooth. Remove from heat. Add the chocolate and stir until melted and smooth. Refrigerate for 20 minutes. In a large bowl, with an electric mixer on medium-high, beat the cream until stiff peaks form. Working quickly, fold the whipped cream into the chilled chocolate mixture, mixing until no traces of white remain. Spoon into the prepared dish. Tap the dish on the counter to remove any air bubbles. Freeze until set, at least 3 hours. Using the foil as handles, transfer the frozen block to a cutting board. Cut into 24 squares. If using graham crackers, break them in half. Sandwich the chocolate squares between the sugar cookies or graham crackers. (You can place the sandwiches on a platter, cover, and return them to the freezer for up to 2 days.) Serve immediately.

what to sip

Two kinds of bubbly cocktails—one spiked and one not—will delight all the guests (including the pregnant ones). And, for a more unexpected treat, mix up a batch of deliciously creamy rum-infused rice milk (yes, rice milk).

CINNAMON RICE MILK

hands-on time: 5 minutes • total time: 2 hours, 5 minutes (includes chilling)

2	32-ounce containers unflavored rice milk
1/4	cup granulated sugar
1/2	teaspoon ground cinnamon
2	tablespoons dark rum
	Cinnamon sticks

In a saucepan, over low heat, warm the rice milk and sugar, stirring often, until the sugar dissolves. Remove from heat. Stir in the ground cinnamon and rum; let cool. Cover and refrigerate for at least 2 hours and up to 24 hours. Pour into flutes. Garnish with a cinnamon stick.

CRANBERRY-GINGER FIZZES

In a large pitcher, combine one 2-liter bottle ginger ale and 2 cups cranberry juice cocktail, both chilled. Pour into flutes.

PASSION FRUIT SPARKLERS

Spoon about 1 tablespoon chilled passion fruit juice into each flute. Add enough chilled Prosecco to fill the glass 3/4 full.

A successful shower game is easy to play, appeals to all ages, and does not overly embarrass the honoree (or, worse, her mother).

who's who?

If you're throwing a baby shower, ask each guest to bring a photograph of herself as an infant. String the pictures along a wall with a clothesline and pins, and have guests try to decipher one adorable face from the next. You can keep it casual and have guests point out their pictures as they walk down the line. Or, to make a true game out of it, number the clothespins and have guests write down guesses as to which pin is holding whose photo. Keep a master list and act as judge. Added benefit: The clothesline doubles as a sweet decoration, and you can hang some of the cute shower loot—onesies, booties, bibs— on the line when the honoree is opening her gifts.

gift bingo

Create enough bingo cards for everyone, as simple or as elaborate as you like (sheets of paper with grids of five boxes by five boxes drawn on them will work just fine). Then have guests write in each square a gift they think the honoree will receive (with the exception of the free center square). As presents are opened (picnic basket! Moses basket!), guests can note their correct guesses with stickers or markers. The first person to get bingo wins.

address yourself

Make the thank-you–note process a little easier on the guest of honor. Ask her to provide you with a batch of her favorite thank-you cards (enough for all the guests at the shower), or buy a nice set for her yourself. Then, as she's opening gifts, instruct each guest to write down her address on one of the thank-you–note envelopes. Have the honoree take the envelopes home so she can express her gratitude faster— without flipping through the White Pages.

gift that gives back

For wedding showers where the guest list includes only close friends and family, introduce a white elephant into the mix: Ask the invitee who was most recently married to bring her most atrocious wedding present to pass along to the bride-to-be. (Make certain, of course, that the giver of that beef-jerky–making kit is not attending.) The guest of honor can then pass on her most atrocious wedding gift (velvet Elvis, anyone?) to the next lucky bride-to-be.

A Shower WRAP-UP

Opening the presents is the easy part. Helping the honoree pack them back up—and doing it quickly and efficiently—is more challenging.

group them

Arrange the gifts in labeled shopping bags or boxes according to type (baby clothes in one, toys in another; linens in one, kitchenware in another). When the honoree arrives home, she'll have an easier time unpacking all the loot.

carry them

When a shopping bag is stuffed with presents, it can be difficult to grasp both handles at once. Make it easier to carry the bag by fashioning a sturdy handle out of packing tape. Cut a 16-inch strip of tape and fold it in half lengthwise, adhesive sides in, so that it is still 16 inches long but half as wide (and not sticky to the touch). Thread the strip through the bag's handles. Tie the ends of the strip above the handle and seal them together with more tape. This loop is your new handle.

ship them

If the guest of honor lives in another town, have a supply of shipping boxes and labels on hand so the gifts can be sent directly from your house to hers. That way, she won't get stuck with excess-baggage fees on her flight—or a car too full of boxes to fit the people she's traveling with.

stuff them

Don't have an economy-size carton of packing peanuts stashed in your garage? Then use the discarded wrapping and tissue paper from the opened presents to cushion fragile items before the guest of honor lugs them home. (Even if the breakables are nestled safely in individual boxes, stuff extra padding between boxes to safeguard against jostling.)

chapter 5

Milestone Birthday

When you think back to childhood birthdays, what do you remember most? Chances are, it's not the presents or the parties (though those were nice, too). It's the magical feeling you had— like you were queen for the day. The next time someone special celebrates a big birthday, why not help her recapture that magic? This party revisits the whimsy of childhood, with everything from cupcakes to penny candy. Queen for the day, indeed.

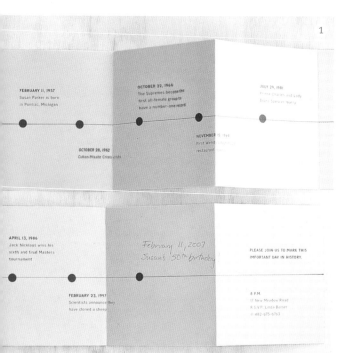

1

FEBRUARY 11, 1957
Susan Parker is born
in Pontiac, Michigan

OCTOBER 22, 1966
The Supremes become the
first all-female group to
have a number-one record

JULY 29, 1981
Prince Charles and Lady
Diana Spencer marry

OCTOBER 28, 1962
Cuban Missile Crisis ends

NOVEMBER 15, 1996
First Wendy's
restaurant

APRIL 13, 1986
Jack Nicklaus wins his
sixth and final Masters
tournament

February 11, 2007
Susan's 50th birthday

PLEASE JOIN US TO MARK THIS
IMPORTANT DAY IN HISTORY.

FEBRUARY 23, 1997
Scientists announce they
have cloned a sheep

8 P.M.
17 New Meadow Road
R.S.V.P. Linda Bauer
(l) 482-675-6763

1. personal history

Create a time line featuring the funniest, most important, or oddest happenings over the course of the birthday person's life (first day of first grade, Red Sox win the World Series). Make the final event the party itself.

2. attack of the clones

Here's a combination invitation and mask—perfect for a surprise party. Make color copies of a photo of the guest of honor's face, then cut the copies out and glue them to Popsicle sticks. Write the party information on the back of each mask, along with a note asking guests to bring the masks to greet the honoree.

3. print-and-mail template

It's time to branch out from the typical birthday invitation (you know, the one with the over-the-hill joke). This clever card marks the passing of years in a more unexpected way. Download the template from www.realsimple. com/celebrations, fill in the party details, and use an arrow to point out the (approximate) tree ring that corresponds with the honoree's age.

when to send

Mail birthday invitations a few weeks in advance. And if the party is a surprise, be sure to clearly mark this on the invitation so there are no slip-ups.

2

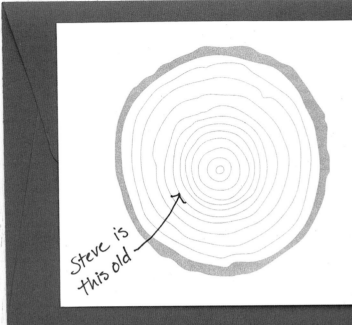

COME CELEBRATE ANOTHER YEAR OF GROWTH!

Saturday, September 22
DATE
6:30 p.m.
TIME
9 Briarfield Road
PLACE
Ellie O'Neill, 431-253-9007
R.S.V.P.

Steve is this old

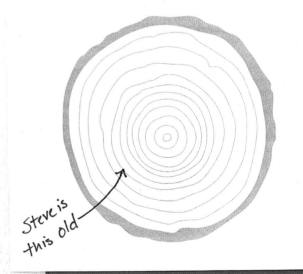

COME CELEBRATE ANOTHER YEAR OF GROWTH!

Saturday, September 22
DATE
6:30 p.m.
TIME
9 Briarfield Road
PLACE
Ellie O'Neill, 431-253-9007
R.S.V.P.

Steve is this old

1. lemon drops

Freeze mint leaves, citrus wedges, maraschino cherries, and ginger slices inside ice cubes to dress up (and cool down) glasses of sparkling water. Guests can mix and match the flavors however they like.

2. here's the scoop

The night before the party, spoon ice cream into muffin tins lined with paper baking cups, then transfer the tins to the freezer. That way, when it's time to serve the cake (or in the case of this party, cupcakes; see page 98), you can simply remove the scoops from the baking cups and drop the ice cream onto waiting plates.

3. lantern chandelier

Why spend the afternoon blowing up a bouquet of balloons from a rented helium tank? Hang a cluster of inexpensive paper lanterns from the ceiling instead. Not only are they more dramatic and interesting but they can also be stored flat and reused anytime.

4. sweet memories

Your guests will feel like kids in a candy store—literally—when you fill goody bags with nostalgic treats like Mary Jane and Bit-O-Honey pieces and those Candy Buttons you used to love biting off the paper. Oh, come on! You're 30 (or 40 or 50 or 60) only once.

3. cheery blossoms

Stand up simple, sturdy blooms, like daisies or tulips, in mismatched soda bottles, then place them around the table in casual clusters for a bit of fresh decor—and recycling savvy.

4. wishes for everyone

Why should just the birthday person get to blow out candles? Let your guests make wishes on their own cupcakes. Roll up paper napkins, tie with a ribbon, then slip in a candle and a match. (Supply a large box of matches to use as a communal striker.)

1. this is your life

Cover the table with a white paper tablecloth, then use a paint pen or a colored marker to note historic or personal events from the honoree's lifetime. (These can be the same events featured in the time-line invitation on page 92.) If you wish, you can also incorporate photographs or drawings representing the events.

2. display cakes

A vertical arrangement of different-size bakery or gift boxes makes an eye-catching stand for cupcakes. Top two of the cupcakes with number candles for the honoree's age (or use four and spell out the birth year).

Milestone Birthday FOOD & DRINK

With surprising flavors and fresh embellishments, basic cupcakes—made from boxed cake mix—become fanciful (yet decidedly adult) birthday treats.

yellow cupcakes (in disguise)

Stir-and-bake vanilla cupcakes from a mix taste significantly less "plain vanilla" when they're gussied up in one of the following ways:

GRAND MARNIER CUPCAKES

Substitute 1/4 cup Grand Marnier (or some other orange liqueur) for 1/4 cup of the water in the package directions and add 1 teaspoon grated orange zest to the batter.

VANILLA BEAN CUPCAKES

Scrape the seeds from 1 vanilla bean into the batter and stir in 1 teaspoon vanilla extract.

CARROT CUPCAKES

Add 1 1/2 cups grated carrots, 1 teaspoon ground cinnamon, and 1/2 teaspoon ground ginger to the batter.

CITRUSY CUPCAKES

Stir the grated zest (but not the bitter white pith beneath) of 1 orange or 2 lemons into the batter.

chocolate cupcakes (in disguise)

With a scoop of this or a shot of that, devil's food cake mix will never again be described as "that old standby."

COCONUT CHOCOLATE CUPCAKES

Add 1 teaspoon coconut extract and 1 cup lightly toasted sweetened shredded coconut to the batter. (To toast the coconut, scatter it on a baking sheet and toast in a 350° F oven until golden, 3 to 5 minutes. Watch carefully: It goes from toasted to scorched in seconds.)

CHOCOLATE AMARETTO CUPCAKES

Substitute 1/4 cup amaretto for 1/4 cup of the water in the package directions and add 1/2 teaspoon almond extract to the batter.

PEANUT BUTTER CHOCOLATE CUPCAKES

Use peanut butter (preferably chunky) in place of the oil in the package directions.

ESPRESSO CUPCAKES

Substitute 1/4 cup Kahlúa for 1/4 cup of the water in the package directions and add 1 tablespoon instant espresso powder to the batter.

chocolate sour-cream icing

hands-on time: 20 minutes • total time: 50 minutes

12	ounces semisweet chocolate—grated, chopped, or chips
1	stick unsalted butter
1	cup sour cream
1	teaspoon vanilla extract
	Pinch kosher salt
$5^{1}/_{2}$ to 6	cups confectioners' sugar

In a saucepan or in a microwave on low heat, warm the chocolate and butter until melted and smooth. Transfer to a large bowl; let cool. Add the sour cream, vanilla, and salt. With an electric mixer on medium, beat the mixture until light and fluffy. Reduce speed to low and slowly add the confectioners' sugar, $1/2$ cup at a time until the desired consistency is reached. Increase speed to medium-high and beat for 1 minute. Cover and refrigerate for at least 30 minutes and up to 8 hours before using. Frost the cupcakes just before serving.

vanilla sour-cream icing

hands-on time: 10 minutes • total time: 40 minutes

2	sticks unsalted butter, at room temperature
$2/3$	cup sour cream, chilled
1	teaspoon vanilla extract
6	cups confectioners' sugar

In a large bowl, with an electric mixer on medium, beat the butter and sour cream until smooth, about 2 minutes. Add the vanilla and mix until combined. Reduce speed to low and slowly add the confectioners' sugar, $1/2$ cup at a time. Increase speed to medium-high and beat for 1 minute. Cover and refrigerate for at least 30 minutes and up to 8 hours before using. Frost the cupcakes just before serving.

grown-up decorations

For the final touch on your creative confections, try one of these pretty trimmings.
- Sliced almonds
- Ice cream sprinkles
- Pastel M&M's or some other candies
- Shaved chocolate
- Edible flowers (such as pansies or Johnny-jump-ups)
- Colored sugar
- Toasted coconut

what to sip

Why not keep the drinks as streamlined and simple as the food? Stock a tub or a cooler with bottles of sparkling water and wine. Any sweet bubbly will work, such as an inexpensive Italian Moscato d'Asti or Spumante—and for extra significant birthdays, a pricier French Demi-Sec.

Here she is
our own Julie McCoy!

Staging a few modern amusements for your guests will ensure that they get more out of the party than a brief (if intense) sugar rush.

read my quips

Ask each guest to bring a picture of the honoree to the party (formal, funny, or otherwise). Place a photo album, a stack of index cards, and a pen on a table near the entrance to the party and instruct each guest to write a clever caption on an index card relating to his or her photo. Slide the card and the photo into facing pages of the album. At the end of the night, the honoree will have a permanent—and, with luck, humorous— memory to take home.

making predictions

What will the honoree be up to on her next mile-stone (you know, the next birthday that ends with a zero)? Have guests write down predictions—from the completely credible to the totally out-there— and stick them in the photo album. Or invite guests to write their predictions on the paper tablecloth, for the rest of the party to enjoy.

insider information

Ask each guest to write down a trivia question based on something he or she knows about the birthday person that no one else does. Whoever can stump the crowd with a question is the winner. Or, before the party, ask the honoree for a few inter-esting personal facts—an odd middle name, a secret wish—and write each one on a slip of paper. Write down several other odd "facts" about the per-son that are not true, then mix all the slips of paper together. At the party, read each slip aloud and have guests guess whether they are true or false.

six degrees of separation

Create your own version of the celebrity-connections game. Choose several random places, people, or things and have guests try to link them to the hon-oree in six steps or less. For example, start with the state of Pennsylvania. Villanova University is located in Pennsylvania; the wildcat is the mascot of Villanova University; the wildcat is also the mascot of Wingate Elementary School in North Carolina; and the birthday boy attended Wingate. *Ta-dah!*

Milestone Birthday ETIQUETTE

From slips of the tongue to slips with the gifts, the following strategies will help you deal with all sorts of birthday-party blunders.

How do I avoid spilling the beans when I'm invited to a surprise party? And what should I do if I—*gulp!*—spill the beans anyway?

If you're the type of person who can't keep anything—your love life, your salary—to yourself, begin planning a stay-quiet strategy as soon as a surprise-party invitation hits your mailbox. As the party approaches, the best thing to do is limit contact with the guest of honor. You should also prepare a credible and airtight excuse in case she asks about your plans for that evening—for example, that you are visiting your parents out of state or having dinner with a friend she has never met.

If you've already let the cat out of the bag, you can't stuff it back in again, but you should still handle it with care. Try to keep the host from knowing you've blown the surprise so the party won't be ruined for her as well. (Consider making a deal with the would-be surprisee that neither of you will tell the host about your mistake.) If the host does find out, do your best to make up for it by offering to help her prepare for the party.

To open gifts, or not to open gifts? That is the question.

It depends. For parties where guests are expected to bring gifts (and do), the birthday honoree should acknowledge their generosity by thanking them in a toast, but she doesn't have to open the gifts during the party unless she wants to. On the other hand, if it was specifically requested in the invitation that guests not bring gifts but some nevertheless did (they always do), the honoree should set the gifts aside, thank the givers for bringing them, and open them afterward. That way, the guests who adhered to the invitation's request won't feel sheepish.

Can I regift a present I received?

Despite what you may think, regifting does have a place in polite society—but it should be used sparingly and with caution. This is not license to pass along every jar of bath salts or pair of flannel pajamas you've unwrapped over the course of a year. But if you've received a nice bottle of Champagne and you don't drink, for example, this type of gift is game for being passed along, provided that a few caveats are met. The first is that you think the person receiving the gift will like it. It should be something you would just as readily have plucked from a store shelf as from the shelf in the back of your closet. Second, the gift should look brand-new and be in its original, undamaged packaging. Third, the person who originally gave you the gift should not be remotely acquainted with the person you're regifting to (and therefore will never spot that handpainted cheese platter at a future potluck). Perhaps most important, always remember to check a potential regift thoroughly for any engravings, monograms, or other dead giveaways that you're really just, well, giving things away.

Is it necessary to write thank-you cards to guests who attended my birthday party? Or should I send them only to those people who brought me a gift?

You should thank anyone who presents you with a gift, birthday or otherwise, but only casual acquaintances require cards. (If the gift game from a close friend or a relative, a phone call or a warm in-person thanks will generally suffice.) A thank-you card should go out within one week of your receiving the gift and should refer specifically to the gift and how you're enjoying it. ("I played the CD you gave me during a recent dinner party, and it set just the right mood. Thank you so much.") You don't need to send a card thanking someone for merely attending your party or for bringing you a minor hostess gift (like a potted plant or a bottle of wine).

toast from the host

When you're making a toast for a milestone birthday, spend some time reflecting on the person's life and accomplishments, whether it was graduating at the top of his class or being a great dad. And try to include some personal anecdotes (about past birthdays, say). But think twice before cracking wise about someone's age—or at least don't dwell on it. Even if the honoree is putting on a happy face, he may not be thrilled with another year under his belt.

Milestone Birthday WRAP-UP

Send each guest home with good memories and one last cupcake (or two). Then transform the rest of the leftovers into delicious second acts.

they've been framed

Stumped about what to give the guest of honor for her birthday? Just frame the party invitation. Buy an appropriate-size frame from a housewares or art-supply store, glue the invitation to the mat provided, and place everything back in the frame. (Note: If the invitation is white, help it stand out by first gluing the invitation to a piece of colored construction paper, trimming the construction paper to leave a small border of color all around, then adhering the invitation and border to the mat.)

handy candy

If your eyes were bigger than your guest list when you purchased that penny candy, there are a few easy ways to eat up the leftovers (that is, without actually eating them).

• When wrapping a gift, use a candy necklace in place of a ribbon.
• Loop those paper strips of Candy Buttons around napkins to make colorful napkin rings.
• Melt Bit-O-Honey pieces for a rich caramel sauce to spoon over ice cream. (Eat it quickly—before the sauce hardens.)
• Save the most nonperishable items (such as Dum Dum Pops) for doling out on Halloween.

frost bites

Stuck with a surplus of cupcakes, even after the guests take some home? (See Takeaway Cupcakes, right.) Then freeze them; they'll keep for up to two months.

• Place the cupcakes on a tray and tightly wrap the entire tray with two layers of plastic wrap. (To avoid disturbing the icing, first place the tray unwrapped in the freezer for 30 minutes to allow the icing to harden.)
• When you're ready to eat the cupcakes, remove them from the freezer and loosen the wrapping. Let unfrosted cakes thaw at room temperature for two to three hours before frosting and eating (or just eating). Place frosted ones in the refrigerator to thaw overnight.

takeaway cupcakes

Even healthy eaters will be happy to have a spare cupcake for a midnight snack at home. Place one on a sturdy paper plate, stick a candle in the center, and cover with plastic wrap. (The candle keeps the wrap from smearing the pretty frosting.) Since there is sour cream in the icing, tell guests to refrigerate the cupcakes if they're not going to eat them right away.

chapter 6 Summer Barbecue

It's no wonder that Shakespeare compared his love to a summer's day. After all, there is perhaps nothing more inspiring. And while the Bard ultimately found his muse to be more lovely and more temperate, he might have reconsidered if this backyard barbecue had been in the picture. With fuss-free dishes, laid-back activities for both kids and adults, and the fastest cleanup imaginable (just throw everything away!), this party is destined to become an instant classic.

Summer Barbecue INVITATIONS

1. play it cool

Here's a refreshing idea the kids can help with. Have them cut Popsicle shapes from colored construction paper, then glue the cutouts to Popsicle sticks after you've written in the barbecue details. Let the invitations dry before sliding them into tall envelopes.

2. have a ball

Let your friends put all their hot air to good use by blowing up these mini–beach-ball invitations. Inflate the balls (sold at party-supply stores) and use a permanent marker to add the party information. Let the ink dry and deflate the balls. Fold them up and mail in small padded envelopes.

3. print-and-mail template

For a hot party during the dog days of summer, go to www.realsimple.com/celebrations and print out this cool canine cartoon. Dash off the details on the lines below, along with a suggestion for what guests can bring to round out the refreshments.

when to send

Mail barbecue invitations at least two to three weeks in advance, or a week earlier if you're planning to host the gathering on a major holiday weekend.

HOT DOG!

IT'S SUMMER. AND WE'RE HAVING A BARBECUE.

DATE Sunday, July 8

TIME 2 p.m. to 6 p.m.

PLACE the Wilsons' backyard
72 Ferry Lane

PLEASE BRING A six-pack of soda and beer

1. beverage cart

Keep the basic white cooler for the beach (or the lemonade stand; see page 122). For your barbecue, fill a child's wagon with ice and stock it with sodas, beer, and bottled water. Bonus: The wagon can be rolled around the yard from time to time for a bit of hammock-side service.

2. night lights

When the sun begins to set but the party's still hopping, scatter Mason jars filled with white votive candles—a more casual take on hurricane lamps—around the yard.

3. summer survival kit

Nothing kills an outdoor party like the arrival of bloodthirsty mosquitoes. So stock sand pails with insect repellent, along with other essentials, like sunscreen and bandages (for the inevitable skinned knees), and place the pails in key spots around the yard. If you find they tip over easily, put stones in the bottoms to weigh them down.

4. grill prep

Just prior to the guests' arrival, heat the grill (or let the coals burn) for 10 to 15 minutes, then go over the grate with a stiff wire grill brush or a ball of crumpled foil held with long-handled tongs.

1. can it

Set out utensils and napkins in rinsed Campbell's soup cans. You'll keep everything orderly while adding a soupçon (sorry) of color to your spread. Just be sure that the rims don't have any jagged edges.

2. on a roll

A long sheet of inexpensive butcher or kraft paper is the ultimate disposable table covering. Dress it up with a runner cut from a roll of wrapping paper and tape down all the edges. If you like, use pinking shears to give the runner a decorative edge, or add colored dot stickers to the butcher paper.

3. support system

Heaping an ear of corn and a hefty burger onto a flimsy paper plate is a recipe for disaster. Nestling that plate into an upturned Frisbee, however, will not only give guests a sturdier surface to eat from but they'll also get a fun favor to take home.

4. protect and serve

From the "Why didn't someone think of this sooner?" file: An inverted mesh colander keeps flies from landing on the buns. And labeled Popsicle sticks help guests distinguish medium burgers from medium-rare.

well

...ll

rare

rare

medium rare

medium well

medium rare

Summer Barbecue FOOD & DRINK

When it comes to barbecue foods, there's nothing better than the tried-and-true, right? Wrong. These recipes take the standard fare to another level.

chunky guacamole

hands-on time: 10 minutes • total time: 10 minutes

3 avocados, halved and pitted
  Juice of 1 lime
1/2 medium red onion, finely chopped
1 jalapeño, seeded and finely chopped
1/2 cup fresh cilantro leaves, roughly chopped
1/2 teaspoon kosher salt
1/4 teaspoon black pepper
  Tortilla chips

In a large bowl, combine the avocados, lime juice, onion, jalapeño, cilantro, salt, and pepper, using a fork to mash the avocado to the desired consistency. (You can cover the guacamole, pressing plastic wrap directly onto the surface, and refrigerate for several hours.) Serve with the tortilla chips.

lemonade remade

hands-on time: 10 minutes • total time: 10 minutes

1 1/2 cups fresh lemon juice
  (from about 12 lemons)
1/2 cup granulated sugar
1 lemon, thinly sliced

In a large pitcher, combine the lemon juice, sugar, and 1 cup cold water. Stir until the sugar dissolves. (You can refrigerate the mixture for several hours.) Add 5 more cups cold water, the lemon slices, some ice, and serve.

Give this basic recipe to the kids. Then make a separate batch for the adults and stir in one of the following thirst-quenching additions:
• 1 cup torn fresh mint leaves and 2 12-ounce cans club soda
• 2 6-ounce cans frozen pineapple juice, defrosted; 1 12-ounce can apricot nectar; and 2 12-ounce cans ginger ale
• 3 cups seeded and pureed watermelon
• 1 cup vodka, chilled
• 1 quart fresh strawberries, hulled, and 1 cup heavy cream (puree together before adding to the lemonade)

go-to burgers

hands-on time: 20 minutes • total time: 30 minutes

2^1/$_2$ to 3 pounds ground beef
^{1}/$_2$ teaspoon kosher salt
^{1}/$_4$ teaspoon black pepper
6 to 8 hamburger buns, split

Lettuce leaves, sliced tomatoes, pickles, ketchup, mustard, salsa, ranch dressing, prepared horse-radish, pesto, and other condiments

Potato chips (optional)

In a large bowl, combine the beef, salt, and pepper. Shape the mixture into 6 to 8 one-inch-thick patties. (You can cover and refriger-ate the meat for up to 8 hours.) Heat grill to medium. Place the patties over direct heat, close the lid, and cook, turning once, to the de-sired doneness, about 10 minutes total for medium. Transfer to the buns and serve with the various toppings and condiments and po-tato chips (if using).

not-exactly-classic corn on the cob

hands-on time: 10 minutes • total time: 15 minutes

6 to 8 ears sweet corn, shucked
4 tablespoons unsalted butter, melted
^{1}/$_2$ teaspoon kosher salt
^{1}/$_4$ teaspoon black pepper

Bring a large pot of water to a boil. Cook the corn until just tender, 3 to 5 minutes. Drain and transfer to a serving dish. Pour the butter over the corn and sprinkle with the salt and pepper, turning to coat. Serve steaming hot. (For other serving options, see New Takes on Corn on the Cob, right.)

grilled sausages

hands-on time: 5 minutes • total time: 15 minutes

12 to 16 sausage links (pork or chicken, sweet or spicy, or a mix)
Crusty bread or rolls (optional)

Heat grill to medium. Place the sausages over indirect heat and grill, turning occasionally, until cooked through, 10 to 15 minutes. (You can cook the sausages over any part of the grill, wherever space allows. If they're over direct heat, cook for a few minutes less.) Serve on the bread or rolls (if using).

new takes on
CORN ON THE COB

Four other versions for your guests to sink their teeth into.

- Roll the corn in ^{1}/$_2$ cup fresh parsley leaves, roughly chopped, after pouring on the butter and sprinkling with the salt and pepper.

- Drizzle the corn with warm garlic butter. (To make: Add 2 finely chopped cloves garlic to the butter before melting it in a sauce pan or in the microwave.)

- Omit the butter, salt, and pepper and instead serve the corn with a sprinkle of cayenne pepper and lime wedges for squeezing.

- Omit the butter and instead coat the corn with extra-virgin olive oil and ^{1}/$_4$ cup fresh basil, roughly chopped.

new takes on

S'MORES

Before sandwiching your s'more with that second graham-cracker square, top the marshmallows and chocolate with one more goody.

• Fresh whole raspberries or sliced strawberries

• Creamy or crunchy peanut butter

• Sliced bananas

grapefruit and cabbage slaw

hands-on time: 10 minutes • total time: 10 minutes

5 cups shredded red cabbage
2 3/4 teaspoons kosher salt
1 large jicama, cut into long strips (optional)
4 scallions (white and green parts), thinly sliced
1/3 cup fresh mint leaves, roughly chopped
2 grapefruit
Juice of 1 lime
2 tablespoons honey
2 tablespoons olive oil
1/8 teaspoon black pepper

In a large bowl, combine the cabbage, 6 cups cold water, and 2 teaspoons of the salt. Let stand for 10 minutes. Drain the cabbage and return to bowl. Add the jicama (if using), scallions, and mint. Peel each grapefruit, then, with a paring knife, cut the segments from their surrounding membranes, working over the bowl to catch any juice. Add the segments to bowl. In a separate bowl, whisk together the lime juice, honey, oil, pepper, and the remaining salt. Pour over the slaw and toss. Let stand for 10 minutes before serving. (You can cover and refrigerate the slaw for up to several hours.)

s'mores with more

hands-on time: 10 minutes • total time: 10 minutes

16 plain, chocolate, or cinnamon graham crackers
4 1.5-ounce milk or dark chocolate bars, broken into pieces
32 large marshmallows (from 1 10-ounce bag)
Wooden skewers

Heat grill to medium-low. Break the crackers in half to form squares. Place the crackers on a platter and top half the squares with the chocolate pieces; set aside. Place some marshmallows on wooden skewers. Hold the skewers over the grill and heat until the marshmallows are puffed and lightly browned on all sides, about 3 minutes. Arrange 2 marshmallows on each chocolate-topped square. Sandwich with the remaining crackers. (To sweeten this recipe further, see New Takes on S'mores, far left.)

He graduated. She ran a marathon. What the heck—it's Saturday night. These hassle-free gatherings work for every season and every reason (even if there actually is no real reason). After all, who needs an excuse to have a party when the planning is so painless?

chapter 7 Cheese Party

If you don't consider yourself a whiz at entertaining, think cheese. Pulling off this sharp-looking spread takes just one trip to the grocery store and the wine shop, a couple of crafty ideas, and a little artful arranging. What's more, the party is all-purpose, meaning it's your ace in the hole for any occasion. No matter how you slice it, this surefire game plan is guaranteed to leave guests smiling.

Cheese Party INVITATIONS

1. a great vintage
Raise the bar with a wine-themed invitation. In place of the winery's name, use yours; for the vintage year, insert the party date; and for the bottling location, provide your address.

2. drink up
Here's an idea that's both memorable and multitasking: Affix a sticker to the center of a blank cardboard coaster that reads, YOUR GLASS HERE, then write the party details on the back. (Blank coasters are sold at party-supply websites, and printable stickers can be found at stationery shops.)

3. print-and-mail template
This invitation gets the point across without being too cheesy. Go to www.realsimple.com/celebrations and print the template onto a piece of yellow or orange card stock. Fill in all the specifics, punch out some Swiss holes, and mail.

when to send
An invitation for a cheese party should ideally be mailed three weeks in advance. But if your event is slightly more impromptu, it's fine to mail the card about a week ahead, or adapt the lines from one of the ideas here to use in an e-mail invitation. (Note: If you are mailing cards out on short notice, sending a save-the-date e-mail beforehand allows guests a bit more time to plan.)

say cheese

TO Casey & Greg

JOIN The Thomases

FOR WINE, CHEESE + CHATTER

WHEN October 6th

WHERE 172 Adams Point Road

TIME 6 p.m.

RSVP BEFORE October 3rd

BY PHONE 929-757-0074

BY E-MAIL thomase@myemail.com

1. pit stops

Spare guests from toting around used napkins and olive pits all night (or, heaven forbid, hiding them in a potted plant). Position yellow gift bags around the party for stashing trash. To keep with the cheese theme, punch a few holes in the bags before setting them out.

2. beverage buddies

Set stacks of coasters, like the ones used for the invitations on page 132, on tables throughout the party. They'll serve as informal decorations, charming party favors, and the only thing standing between you and a roomful of permanently ringed surfaces.

3. stuck on you

Place a whole lemon or orange here and there for guests to poke tooth-picks into. Stick in a couple of picks yourself to start things off and attach a USED PICKS HERE label to ensure everyone gets the message.

4. the big chill

Make a water bath to cool sparkling and white wines quickly: Fill the kitchen sink or a bucket halfway with ice. Then add water and a handful of salt. Submerge bottles for at least 10 minutes before guests arrive.

Cheese Party THE TABLE

1. bread winners
To create an elegant and edible centerpiece, bundle baguettes in large vases and group bread sticks in smaller ones (or even drinking glasses).

2. knife pointers
You'll need three different tools to serve the full range of cheeses: a butter knife for soft cheeses, like Brie; a paring knife for semihard varieties, like blue cheese and Cheddar; and a cheese plane for aged and hard wedges, like Parmigiano-Reggiano and Mimolette.

3. mix and match
Don't have 24 identical serving plates? Don't worry. Just gather all your small plates and stack them on the table for a chic-without-trying-too-hard effect. If you still don't have enough small plates to go around, pick up some funky mismatched dishes from an antique shop or borrow a set from a neighbor or a friend.

4. making introductions
For those who don't know jack about cheese, write the name and a description of each type you're serving on a HELLO, MY NAME IS label attached to a toothpick. Then position the cheeses on a slate, marble, or wooden board.

4

Cheese Party FOOD & DRINK

Though the nursery rhyme says that the cheese stands alone, it's much more interesting when accompanied by olives, fruits, and, yes, wine.

menu

ALL RECIPES SERVE 6 TO 8

crowd-pleasing cheese platter

citrus olives

cream cheese with pepper jelly

pickled carrots

baked Brie

modern cheese balls

white and red wines

crowd-pleasing cheese platter

To assemble a well-balanced cheese plate, pick one variety from each of the categories below (allow 1/3 to 1/2 pound of cheese total per person). Include at least one familiar cheese so even the most unadventurous eaters will sample the spread. Remove your cheeses from the refrigerator an hour before serving (cold mutes flavor), and serve them with baguettes, bread sticks, crackers, nuts, dried and fresh fruit, and the dishes that follow.

SOFT AND CREAMY
Brillat-Savarin, goat cheese, Constant Bliss.

BLUE AND BOLD
Stilton, Valdeón, Mountain Gorgonzola.

SEMIHARD AND SMOOTH
Cheddar, Comté, Gouda.

AGED AND RICH
Manchego, Mimolette, Parmigiano-Reggiano.

You can also find these cheese categories on the *Real Simple* Party by Numbers wheel, on the inside back cover.

citrus olives

hands-on time: 5 minutes • total time: 1 hour, 5 minutes (includes marinating)

  1 pint (2 cups) green olives
    Zest from 1 lemon, cut into thin strips
  1 bay leaf
  1/4 cup extra-virgin olive oil

In a serving bowl, combine the olives, lemon zest, bay leaf, and oil. Set aside at room temperature, stirring occasionally, for at least 1 hour and up to 24 hours before serving.

cream cheese with pepper jelly

hands-on time: 5 minutes • total time: 5 minutes

  1 8-ounce package cream cheese
  1 cup jarred pepper jelly or any berry jelly (such as currant)
  2 4.25-ounce boxes water crackers

Place the cream cheese in a serving dish or on a plate. Spread the jelly evenly over the top. (You can cover and refrigerate the jelly-topped cream cheese for a couple of hours.) Serve with the crackers.

pickled carrots

hands-on time: 5 minutes • total time: 3 days
(includes pickling)

1 32-ounce jar pickles
1 pound slender carrots, peeled

Remove the pickles from the jar and transfer to a resealable container. Refrigerate and reserve for another use. Add the carrots to the jar of pickle juice, cutting them to fit if necessary. Screw on the lid and refrigerate for at least 3 days and up to 2 weeks.

baked Brie

hands-on time: 10 minutes • total time: 1 hour,
5 minutes

2 tablespoons light brown sugar
2 tablespoons pecan halves,
   roughly chopped
1 sheet puff pastry
   Flour for the work surface
1 3^1/$_2$-inch wheel Brie (8.5 to 10 ounces)
1 egg, lightly beaten

Heat oven to 400° F. Line a baking sheet with parchment paper or aluminum foil. In a small bowl, combine the sugar and pecans; set aside. Unfold the pastry and place it on a lightly floured work surface. Roll the pastry out to a ^{1}/$_8$-inch thickness. Place the Brie in the center. Spread the pecan mixture over the Brie, being

careful not to spill any on the pastry. Using a sharp knife, cut the pastry into a circle, allowing 4 inches all around the Brie. Fold the pastry over the Brie, allowing it to fall into pleats. Pinch together the extra pastry in the center to seal. Transfer to the baking sheet. (You can cover and refrigerate the pastry-wrapped Brie for up to several hours before baking.) Lightly brush the top of the pastry with the egg. Bake until golden, about 35 minutes. Let cool on the baking sheet for 20 minutes. Transfer to a plate and serve warm.

modern cheese balls

hands-on time: 40 minutes • total time: 40 minutes

1 cup wasabi-coated green peas
5 gingersnap cookies
1 cup granola
^{1}/$_4$ cup (1 ounce) finely grated Parmesan
1 teaspoon whole fennel seeds
1 10.5- or 11-ounce log goat cheese

Grind the peas in a food processor and transfer the crumbs to a plate. Wipe out the bowl of the food processor. Repeat with the gingersnaps, then the granola. Combine the Parmesan and fennel on another plate. Shape the goat cheese into balls, using about 1^1/$_2$ teaspoons for each. Roll the balls in the coatings and transfer to a platter. (You can cover and refrigerate the balls, uncoated, for up to 24 hours. Coat the balls no more than 1 hour before the party.)

what to sip

There are no hard rules when it comes to pairing wine with cheese, but in general whites tend to be more *fromage*-friendly than reds. For worry-free wines that complement all varieties of cheese, stick with Riesling and sparkling wines. If you'd like to add a red to the mix, try a Cabernet Sauvignon with any of the aged and rich cheeses.

Cheese Party ACTIVITIES

Once the wine and the conversation are flowing, all you need to maintain momentum is a spot-on sound track, plus a way to make the memories last.

perfect party playlist

These 40 sure-hit songs will see you through this shindig and most gatherings in general, from warm-up to wind-down. Burn all the tunes in order onto CDs, or download them onto an MP3 player, and you won't have to worry about the music— or any self-appointed DJs— for the entire evening.

THE COCKTAILS BEGIN...

- Nina Simone, "Feeling Good"
- Miles Davis, "Four"
- Tito Puente, "Take That"
- Hugh Masekela, "Grazing in the Grass"
- Bob Marley, "Waiting in Vain"
- Frank Sinatra, "The Way You Look Tonight"
- Swing Out Sister, "Am I the Same Girl"
- Dionne Warwick, "(There's) Always Something There to Remind Me"
- Ray Charles, "Hallelujah I Love Her So"
- Lenny Kravitz, "It Ain't Over Til It's Over"
- Maroon Five, "Sunday Morning"
- George Michael, "Freedom 90"

THE PARTY WARMS UP...

- Stevie Wonder, "Knock Me Off My Feet"
- Rolling Stones, "Superstition"
- The Temptations, "Ain't Too Proud to Beg"
- Natalie Cole, "This Will Be"
- Diana Ross, "I'm Coming Out"
- Cheryl Lynn, "Got to Be Real"
- The Emotions, "Best of My Love"
- Bonnie Pointer, "Heaven Must Have Sent You"
- Stevie Wonder, "Uptight (Everything's Alright)"

THE PARTY IS IN FULL SWING...

- Sugarhill Gang, "Rapper's Delight"
- Soft Cell, "Tainted Love"
- Michael Jackson, "Wanna Be Startin' Somethin'"
- Depeche Mode, "Just Can't Get Enough"
- Lauryn Hill, "Doo Wop (That Thing)"
- Prince, "Raspberry Beret"
- Neil Diamond, "Sweet Caroline"
- Madonna, "Ray of Light"
- The Cure, "Just Like Heaven"

LAST CALL...

- New Order, "Age of Consent"
- U2, "The Sweetest Thing"
- Carly Simon, "You're So Vain"
- The Police, "So Lonely"
- David Bowie, "Changes"
- David Gray, "Babylon"
- Coldplay, "Fix You"
- Rod Stewart, "Maggie May"
- The Cure, "Close to Me"
- Oasis, "Live Forever"

picture this

There's no way you're going to catch every noteworthy moment at your party. Place disposable cameras in a bowl with a sign reading, SAY CHEESE! so guests can record all the highlights.

Cheese Party ETIQUETTE

Dip into these easy strategies for avoiding the common pitfalls of any wine-and-cheese or cocktail party.

My living room looks like a junior-high dance. How do I encourage mingling?

The most effective way is to help people find common ground: "Joe, meet Samantha; Samantha, Joe. Samantha's a huge Yankees fan, too." Repeating names during the introduction helps solidify the memory and reduces the likelihood that guests will have to reintroduce themselves after you've gone. To keep the mixer from grinding to a halt while you're taking coats and restocking the bar, appoint a friend to take over the introductions.

How can I remember, er, what's-his-name?

You're OK, at least, with the people you invited, but with those plus-ones, your mind can go blank. When you meet someone new, say his name in your head three times, then reinforce the memory by using the name in your conversation as soon as possible ("So, Tim, how did you get involved with the museum's events committee?"). You can also try associating the person's name with a distinguishing feature. For example, if you're introduced to a muscular, wide-shouldered fellow named Brad, think "broad Brad."

What's the best way to juggle food and a drink—all while welcoming guests?

Sure, you'll greet your dearest friends with a kiss, but you'll need a dry palm for shaking hands with less familiar guests. To prevent giving anyone an icy-cold (or, worse, cheese-smeared) palm, try this technique: Hold your drink in your left hand with a napkin wrapped around the glass, so you can easily wipe your right hand after sampling the Mimolette. Then use your (clean, dry) right hand for handshakes—and slicing more Mimolette.

As for holding a plate full of food and a drink and partaking of both, the smartest solution is simply not to attempt it. Instead, either sit down to eat or, if you choose to remain standing, set your drink on a nearby table while you sample from the plate. Again, keep a napkin handy to wipe your right hand before you extend it in a greeting.

How can I escape from an interminable conversation?

It's easy to get trapped in a corner with your chattiest guest. Getting out of the situation graciously is more difficult. The savviest tactic is to invite a third person to join the conversation, make a connection between the two of them, and then quietly excuse yourself. As host, you also have a number of built-in excuses: You need to show a guest where the coats are stashed, turn off the oven, or greet a recent arrival. As a last resort, simply say, "Can we continue this conversation in a bit? I need to refill my drink now," and move on to the bar.

Is it OK to serve screw-top or boxed wine at the party?

Absolutely. Thanks to the latest technological advances in the wine industry, vintage-dated varietal wines—yes, the good stuff—are now being sold in more economical and practical screw-top bottles and even boxes. It is unlikely you'll encounter a spoiled bottle of screw-top wine. Boxes have even more going for them: They can hold much greater quantities of wine (about three liters, or four bottles' worth), are easier to transport and more affordable than bottles, and stay fresh longer after opening (about a month as opposed to a traditional bottle's three- to five-day life span). Still feeling squeamish about serving screw-top or boxed wine? Just decant the wine into a glass carafe and your guests will be none the wiser.

How do I know if the wine I've just opened is corked?

Wine experts estimate that 1 in 10 bottles will be corked (contaminated by residue on the cork), so it pays to know when a bottle is tainted. Luckily, the signs are pretty clear. If the wine gives off an aroma of damp newspaper or moldy basement, it is probably corked. And though there's nothing dangerous about drinking corked wine, it's certainly not as pleasurable as drinking good wine, so you'll probably want to pour the bottle down the drain.

toast from the host

Sure, raising a glass may not be typical at this type of party. But if it's a rare occasion to have all your friends gathered in one room, why not salute them? Since most folks will have a glass in hand at any given moment, you only need to wait for a lull in the conversation to speak up. Bear in mind who is in attendance, and don't focus on recounting memories that will be shared by only some party guests. Something inclusive like "May friendship, like wine, improve as time advances, and may we have old wine, old friends, and young cares" makes everyone feel involved and appreciated.

Cheese Party WRAP-UP

Extend the life of your party provisions (and even the corks!) with proper storage techniques and creative ideas for reuse.

the cheese

Different varieties call for different storage methods. Soft cheeses, like Brie and triple-cream, should be stored in resealable plastic containers, while it's best to wrap semihard and aged cheeses, like Cheddar and Parmigiano-Reggiano, first in wax or parchment paper, then in plastic wrap. Blue cheeses should be packaged in plastic alone.

the wine

Reinsert the original cork back into the opened bottle, or use a tight-sealing rubber stopper (available at most wine shops). Store the wine—whether white or red—in the refrigerator, where the cold will help preserve it. Both red and white wine will keep for three to five days. (Unrefrigerated, they will last only a day or two.) Hint: If your wine starts to smell of paint or nail polish, it's time to say, "Au revoir."

the other hors d'oeuvres

Most of the other dishes (for example, the modern cheese balls) won't be as good the second time around. Except, that is, for the olives.

- Toss them with cooked pasta, a generous drizzle of olive oil, plenty of fresh pepper, some grated lemon zest, and any leftover goat cheese you may have on hand. Serve at room temperature.
- Use as a topping for plain chicken or fish: Pat some chopped olives on top of a chicken cutlet or a fillet of white fish, sprinkle with pepper, drizzle with olive oil, and slide under the broiler. Top with chopped fresh parsley and lemon juice before serving.
- Drop them in martinis.

the corks

Save those orphaned stoppers from empty wine bottles—they can be used in a number of different new ways. Poke stud earrings into a cork and toss it in your travel bag; slice one into disks and glue them to the bottoms of furniture to protect floors; wedge a cork under the handle of an uninsulated pot lid to provide a cool grip when working over a hot stove; or use corks as place holders or dish identifiers (see page 54) at your next party.

chapter 8 *Dinner Party*

It's 8 P.M.—do you know where your good dishes are? Gathering dust in the back of the cupboard, no doubt. So why not throw a proper dinner party? It's the perfect excuse for breaking out the china, the crystal, and the silver and celebrating, well, just about anything. With a menu that centers around make-ahead dishes and pretty decorating touches that take virtually no time (or skill), fine dining is easier than you think.

Dinner Party INVITATIONS

You are invited to
dinner at the Springs'

* * *

CITRUS SALAD

* * *

BEEF BOURGUIGNONNE

BROCCOLI RABE WITH RED CURRANT
VINAIGRETTE

GOLDEN-CRUSTED POTATOES

* * *

RUSTIC APPLE TART

* * *

FRIDAY, SEPTEMBER 14
6:30 P.M.
490 RUMSTICK ROAD
736-626-3908

1

1. carte du jour

A menu-style invitation that previews the evening's meal will entice guests to RSVP quickly. Add the date, the time, and the place at the bottom, and back the invitation with a piece of card stock (like the ink-edged piece at left).

2. express yourself

Since a dinner party is about personal touches (the foods you serve, the wine you choose, the music you play), why not add a few to the invitation as well? Buy a set of plain note cards (or use your own stationery) and write a quotation about food, friends, or celebrations on the front.

3. print-and-mail template

This graphic place setting strikes the perfect balance of formality and fun— a reflection of your dinner to come. Go to www.realsimple.com/celebrations to print out the invitation. Then write in your party information and serve it up to your guests.

when to send

An invitation to a dinner party that does not fall near a holiday should be mailed three weeks in advance. If it turns out a couple of guests cannot attend, feel free to extend the invitation to other friends over the phone.

"Sit down and feed,
and welcome to our table."
— William Shakespeare

2

1. mass appeal

To make the dining room glow, group different-size pillar candles together on a side table and wrap each in brown parchment paper. For an extra decorative effect, first punch holes along the top and the bottom of each sheet, then tie with a piece of suede cord (sold at craft stores). Additional sets of candles can go on the coffee table and near the entryway. (Note: Keep an eye on the candles as they burn down, to ensure the paper wrappings don't catch fire.)

2. chart a course

A well-planned seating arrangement can go a long way toward encouraging conversation—and harmony—among your tablemates. To keep things manageable, invite no more than six to eight guests; then seat talkative types next to quiet ones, separate couples, keep the argumentative folks far from one another, and stagger the men and the women.

3. polish up

If you haven't used your china, crystal, and silver in a while—say, since you received them as wedding gifts—they may need some pre-party attention. Wipe the dishes and the crystal with a clean, damp cloth; use silver-polish wipes to remove light tarnish from flatware (use long strokes, not circular ones); and try a foaming silver polish for more serious residue.

4. open sesame

Buy flowers two days early to allow the blossoms to unfold. Speed up the process even more by cutting the stems at an angle and placing them in a bucket of warm water.

Dinner Party THE TABLE

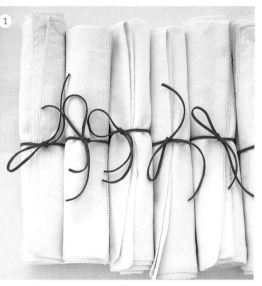

1. knot ready

In place of napkin rings, wrap your linens with the same suede cord used for the pillar candles. Use a bow or a knot; either way, you'll tie the decorating theme together.

2. points of view

Here's a bright idea: Wrap a votive holder in parchment paper (punch holes along the paper's edge if you like), then write an invitee's name on the votive and place it by his seat. If some guests don't know one another, write the names on both sides of the votives so people across the table can see them.

3. of course

Set a dinner menu on each plate detailing the evening's bill of fare. If you used the menu for your invitation (see page 150), just delete the party details before you use it here.

4. conversation starter

Your guests won't have to bob and weave to see around this beautiful but low-profile centerpiece. Buy bunches of the same flower (anything from roses to carnations), trim the stems down to about two inches, then pack a generous number of blooms in clear, shallow vases (or even a Pyrex baking dish or a series of glass loaf pans).

Dinner Party FOOD & DRINK

From the salad to the sweet, all these dishes can be made in advance. Then it's just a matter of tossing, heating, serving, and sitting back.

menu

ALL RECIPES SERVE 6 TO 8

citrus salad

beef bourguignonne

golden-crusted potatoes

broccoli rabe with
red currant vinaigrette

rustic apple tart

red wine

citrus salad

hands-on time: 20 minutes · total time: 20 minutes

- 1/4 cup fresh orange juice
- 1 tablespoon white wine vinegar
- 1 shallot, finely chopped
- 1/2 teaspoon kosher salt
- 1/4 teaspoon black pepper
- 1/4 cup extra-virgin olive oil
- 3 heads Bibb or Boston lettuce,
  rinsed and torn (or substitute 2 5-ounce
  bags mixed salad greens)
- 2 navel oranges, peeled and sliced
  into thin circles
- 3/4 cup (about 3 ounces) pecans, toasted
  and roughly chopped
- 4 ounces goat cheese, crumbled (optional)

In a large bowl, whisk together the orange juice, vinegar, shallot, salt, and pepper. Whisking constantly, slowly add the oil. (You can cover and refrigerate the vinaigrette and salad ingredients separately for up to several hours. Whisk the vinaigrette to recombine just before using.) Add the lettuce, oranges, pecans, and goat cheese (if using) to the vinaigrette and toss.

beef bourguignonne

hands-on time: 1 1/2 hours · total time: 2 1/2 hours

- 3 1/2 to 4 pounds stew or chuck meat, cut
  into 1 1/2-inch pieces
- 1 tablespoon plus 1/4 teaspoon kosher salt
- 1 1/2 teaspoons black pepper
- 3 tablespoons canola oil
- 1 bottle dry red wine (such as
  Côtes du Rhône)
- 1 14.5-ounce can diced tomatoes, drained
- 2 14.5-ounce cans (3 1/2 cups) low-sodium
  chicken broth
- 1/2 small yellow onion
- 1 pound baby-cut carrots
- 8 cloves garlic, peeled
- 3 tablespoons unsalted butter
- 1 pound fresh or frozen pearl onions
- 1 pound button mushrooms, thickly sliced

Heat oven to 300° F. Season the meat on all sides with 1 tablespoon of the salt and the pepper. Heat the oil in a Dutch oven or large ovenproof pot over medium heat. Working in batches, cook the meat until browned on all sides. Transfer to a plate. Add the wine to the drippings in the pot and bring to a boil. Cook for

3 minutes, using a wooden spoon to stir and scrape the bottom of the pot. Add the meat, tomatoes, and 2 cups of the broth. Bring to a simmer. Add the yellow onion, 3 of the baby carrots, and the garlic. Cover tightly and transfer to the oven for 1 hour. Add the remaining carrots, cover, and return to oven until the meat is fork-tender but not falling apart, about 30 minutes more. Skim any fat from the surface.

Meanwhile, melt 1 tablespoon of the butter in a large skillet over medium heat. Add the pearl onions and the remaining broth. Simmer, stirring occasionally, until the liquid almost completely evaporates and the onions are tender, about 15 minutes. Transfer to a plate. Wipe out skillet and return to medium heat. Melt the remaining butter. Add the mushrooms and toss to coat. Cook, stirring occasionally, until the liquid released by the mushrooms almost completely evaporates, about 12 minutes. Transfer to the plate with the onions and add the remaining salt. (You can cover and refrigerate the ingredients, keeping the onions and mushrooms separate from the stew, for up to 2 days. The day of the party, skim any fat from the surface of the stew and reheat, covered, over a medium-low flame for 45 minutes.)

Transfer the pot of stew to the stovetop and warm over medium-high heat. Using a slotted spoon, remove and discard the onion half. Simmer, uncovered, until the stew reduces to the desired consistency, 10 to 20 minutes. Add the pearl onions and mushrooms and simmer for 5 minutes more. Spoon onto plates.

golden-crusted potatoes

hands-on time: 15 minutes • total time: 20 minutes

- 4 pounds russet potatoes, peeled and quartered
- 10 tablespoons unsalted butter, at room temperature
- 1 cup heavy cream
- 2¹/₂ teaspoons kosher salt
- ¹/₄ teaspoon black pepper
- ¹/₂ cup whole milk (optional)

Heat oven to 400° F. Place the potatoes in a large pot. Add enough cold water to cover. Bring to a boil. Reduce heat and simmer until tender, about 15 minutes. Drain the potatoes, return them to pot, and mash. Add 8 tablespoons of the butter, the cream, salt, and pepper and combine. If a thinner consistency is desired, add the milk a few tablespoons at a time. Transfer the potato mixture to a casserole dish and dot with the remaining butter. Bake, uncovered, until the top is crisp and golden, about 30 minutes.

what to do when

1 DAY BEFORE
- Make the beef bourguignonne, cover, and refrigerate.

THE DAY OF THE PARTY
- While it's still early, assemble the ingredients for the salad and the vinaigrette; refrigerate them separately.
- Bake the tart.

2 HOURS BEFORE GUESTS ARRIVE
- Mash the potatoes, transfer them to a baking dish, and set aside at room temperature.

1 HOUR BEFORE GUESTS ARRIVE
- Reheat the beef bourguignonne.
- Transfer the potatoes to oven.

JUST BEFORE DINNER
- Toss the salad.
- Make the broccoli rabe.

Dinner Party FOOD & DRINK

what to sip

Tradition holds that whatever wine goes in the stew should go in the glass. That's fine, but a better match for rich beef stew and bitter broccoli rabe is a flavor-packed Rioja or Syrah.

broccoli rabe with red currant vinaigrette

hands-on time: 10 minutes • total time: 15 minutes

- 3 bunches (about 3 pounds) broccoli rabe
- 1/4 cup red currant jelly
- 1/4 teaspoon red pepper flakes
- 1/2 teaspoon Dijon mustard
- 1/2 teaspoon kosher salt
- 1/8 teaspoon black pepper
- 1/4 cup extra-virgin olive oil

Bring a large pot of salted water to a boil. Add the broccoli rabe and cook until almost tender, about 3 minutes. Drain, squeezing to remove any excess water. Transfer the broccoli rabe to a serving bowl. Heat the jelly in a small saucepan over low heat for 2 to 3 minutes. Remove from heat. Whisk in the red pepper, mustard, salt, and black pepper. Whisking constantly, slowly add the oil. Drizzle the vinaigrette over the broccoli rabe and toss. Serve warm or at room temperature.

rustic apple tart

hands-on time: 20 minutes • total time: 1 1/2 hours

- 1 refrigerated piecrust
- 5 medium apples, preferably Empire or McIntosh, peeled and sliced 1/4 inch thick
- 1/4 cup plus 2 tablespoons granulated sugar
- 1/2 teaspoon ground cinnamon
- 1 teaspoon grated lemon zest

Heat oven to 375° F. Unfold the piecrust and place it on a baking sheet lined with aluminum foil. In a large bowl, combine the apples, 1/4 cup of the sugar, the cinnamon, and lemon zest. Place the apple mixture in the center of the crust. Fold the edge of the crust over the apple mixture, allowing it to fall into pleats (the center of the tart should be uncovered). Lightly brush the top of the crust with water and sprinkle with the remaining sugar. Bake until golden brown, about 40 minutes. Let cool for at least 30 minutes. Serve warm or at room temperature.

The beauty—and the focus—of a dinner party are the food, the drink, and the friendships. Here are a few ways to make the most of all of them.

vine language

If a guest brings you a particularly nice bottle of wine as a hostess gift, write his name on the label. That way, when you eventually pop the cork, you can raise a toast to him and then call or e-mail to say how much you enjoyed the gift.

dish it out

Write slightly strange statements (for example, "My parents have a pet ostrich") on strips of paper and place one under each guest's plate. When everyone is seated, ask your guests to privately read the phrases and try to work them naturally and discreetly into the dinner conversation. Then see who can guess when someone is fibbing. Hint: The game works best if you select phrases that are somehow related to what the group will most likely talk about—politics, jobs, families, travel, etc.

movable feast

You've made it through the before-dinner cocktails, the salad course, and the entrée when you realize you haven't spoken to anyone at the far end of the table. To make sure everyone gets to spend time with everyone else, change the seating arrangement before you serve dessert.

after-hours club

To relieve some of the table-clearing pressure and let the dinner wind down on a less formal note, move the party into the living room once you've finished dessert. Load the place-card votives onto a tray, refilling them with new candles if necessary, and set the tray on the coffee table to echo the dinner table's ambience. Serve guests coffee or after-dinner drinks and, if you wish, some biscotti or bite-size chocolates.

Dinner Party ETIQUETTE

This advice will help you recover from all kinds of dinner-party trip-ups. (Because crawling under the table is not an option.)

Do I have to invite someone to a dinner party because she invited me to hers?

Although your only true obligation as a guest at someone else's dinner party is to let your sparkling personality light up the table, you may still feel as if reciprocation is in order. But there's no need to automatically invite that host to your next gathering. Remember that more important than responding to hospitality in kind is simply responding with kindness: Write a thank-you note telling your host what a great time you had and consider yourselves even.

What should I do if a guest unexpectedly brings another guest?

You open the door to find your final guest standing on your porch...with a friend. Eight place settings, nine hungry people. What now? You may be tempted to offer your own portion of food to the newcomer, but that will make her feel more awkward. Instead, squeeze in an extra place setting at the table (use a kitchen chair and everyday dinnerware if you're out of the fancy stuff); divide the invited guest's portion between the two of them (with humorous apologies); and be sure to pass plenty of side dishes their way.

John's allergic to peanuts, and Nancy doesn't eat meat. I was planning on serving chicken skewers with peanut dipping sauce. Help!

If your guests have hard-line allergies or dietary restrictions, they'll probably inform you of them when they RSVP, and you should do your best to accommodate them. You don't need to redesign the entire menu, but do make sure there is at least one hearty dish they can eat (so they're not nibbling salad all night). If a guest hasn't warned you of her needs in advance, or if it's her dinner companion whose restrictions you didn't know about, try to focus on what you do have to offer rather than on what you don't. Suggest another dish on the table that will work within the guest's limitations and explain how it was prepared (for example, if it was made with vegetable rather than chicken broth).

Is there a secret to pouring wine without dribbling it on the tablecloth?

To pour from any bottle without spillage, follow this easy technique: When you open the wine, don't remove the entire foil capsule. Instead, leave a ridge of foil around the opening of the bottle to catch drips. When you pour, imagine you're using the bottle to shake hands with the guest you're serving: Extend your hand so the label is facing the guest, pour the wine with a downward tilt of the wrist, tilt the bottle back up when you've finished pouring, and immediately twist it clockwise to prevent wine from running down the outside. To wipe up any errant droplets, keep a folded napkin at the ready.

What do I do if I see bits of cork floating in the wine I just poured?

Don't worry. Even the most experienced sommelier sometimes can't prevent small pieces of cork from falling into the bottle when he is opening wine, and the fragments won't affect the flavor of the wine in the glass. You have three choices here: Discreetly fish the crumbs out of the glass with a fork; take the glass as your own; or move on and hope no one notices.

How do I recover from inadvertently insulting someone at the table?

Whether you've just denounced the city's educational system to a public-school teacher or SUVs to a 4x4 driver, your best option is to laugh and gently scold yourself ("Oh dear, insert foot in mouth"). Resist the temptation to automatically apologize, as you'll most likely come off as insincere. Listen politely if the person counters with her philosophy, then move on to a less controversial subject.

toast from the host

An ideal time for a dinner-party toast is just before dessert is served, when everyone is full and happy. See to it that each guest has something to toast with (whether it is wine, coffee, or water), and try a simple line like "To good friends and good conversation— may we never run out of either of them."

Dinner Party WRAP-UP

Sure, you may be tempted to dump everything into the dishwasher and be done with it. But if you care about your best tableware, resist that urge.

the clean routine

You can go ahead and wait until the next day to wash the dishes (after all, who wants dishpan hands at midnight?), but you will need to get sudsy if you want to protect your special-occasion china, crystal, and silver from scratches and breakage. First, remove your rings (diamonds can cut glass), then grab some mild dishwashing liquid and a nonabrasive sponge and work your way up from the most delicate items to the sturdiest, dirtiest pieces.

crystal

Place a rubber mat in the sink to cushion glasses in case they topple. Wash each glass with warm, soapy water, rinse thoroughly, and place on a rack or a towel to air-dry.

china

Wash with a sponge in very hot, soapy water, and change the water often to maintain suds until the last piece. (To remove a coffee or tea stain from the bottom of a cup, swish two tablespoons of white vinegar in it, then wash.) Rinse china thoroughly with hot water and let air-dry if you have room. Otherwise, dry with a cotton cloth.

silver

If sterling-silver utensils were in contact with acidic foods, like salt, mayonnaise, and eggs, it's important to rinse them immediately with hot water to avoid corrosion and discoloration. Then wash them well in warm, soapy water and dry with a cotton cloth or a quilted paper towel.

linens

Eight guests around a table means 16 elbows and 16 ways to knock over a glass of red wine onto your favorite tablecloth. When accidents happen during the meal, ripping the whole thing off and scrubbing furiously is not an option. Instead, dampen a clean sponge with water, add a teaspoon of delicate-wash detergent, and dab it on the red-wine spill to stop the stain in its tracks. Once everyone has gone home, follow up with a more thorough treatment: Rinse the area, cover the stain with salt, stretch the fabric over a bowl, and pour boiling water over it from a height of about one foot.

chapter 9 Dessert Party

Want to experience la dolce vita? Nothing says the sweet life like an indulgent, all-desserts (and all-adults) party. Think about it: One day off the diet won't kill you, and the fact that you can stage this celebration with just a few baking shortcuts up your oven mitt, a couple of far-from-saccharine decorating ideas, and an utterly no-fuss cleanup, well, that's just the icing on the (coconut pudding) cake.

Dessert Party INVITATIONS

1. sweet talk
Turn pink note cards into invitations with an appropriately tempting message. If you like, use cards with a pretty scalloped edge (check specialty stationery stores), or use pinking shears to create an interesting edge yourself.

2. baker's mark
Even if you don't serve Grandma's spice cake, this invitation can lend your party a dash of old-fashioned charm. Write or type all the information on a blank recipe card, and tie a bakery-string bow through a hole punched in the corner.

3. print-and-mail template
Life may be like a box of chocolates, but your dessert-party guests will know just what they're going to get with an invitation inscribed on a map to a chocolate sampler box. Go to www.realsimple.com/celebrations and print out the template. Then jot down the party details in the blank spaces.

when to send
Two weeks should be plenty of notice for a dessert party unless you're in the peak of summer wedding (and therefore shower) season. In that case, allow three weeks.

RASPBERRY
CREAM

**A SWEET
TREAT AWAITS YOU AT...**

Jane's dessert
party

Sunday, May 27
3p.m.
55 Court Street

MEL

R.S.V.P.
581-329-0809

A

1. paper lights

Pink paper cupcake liners turn an ordinary strand of white lights into a string of delicate blossoms. Just cut a small slit through the center of each liner with a knife and poke the bulb through. Then drape the string along a mantel or a table's edge.

2. the ultimate brush-off

Here's a favor your guests will truly use when the party is over: Wrap pretty toothbrushes in clear cellophane, tie the ends with bakery string, and attach a key tag that reads, SWEET-TOOTH RX. Place the brushes in a decorative container, like this silver julep cup, on a table near the door.

3. have a cow

What would a cookie be without milk? If you don't want your guests to find out, fill large ceramic mixing bowls with ice and set old-fashioned glass bottles (or clear plastic containers) of milk in them.

4. pick the pan

Line a jelly-roll pan with waxed paper or gift wrap and use it to neatly store glasses and bundles of utensils. Added benefit: You can use it to transport used glasses to the sink or to display cookies and other sweets (see page 174).

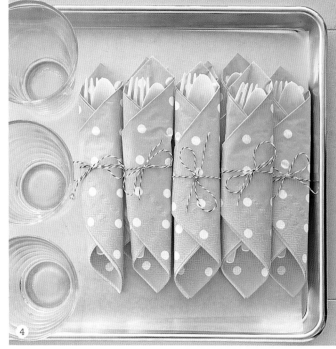

Dessert Party THE TABLE

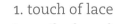

3. metal workers

Along with corralling napkins and glasses, baking tins can hold the sweets. Set out some items in the pans they were made in (like the Coconut Pudding Cake, page 176) and offer up other treats in trays lined with parchment paper (to make cleanup a snap).

4. home plate

There's no need for an expensive florist's arrangement when a glass cake stand can substitute as an on-call centerpiece. Place peonies or your flower of choice (cut the stems short first) on the plate, pour in a small amount of water, and see the dish rise to the occasion. (The flowers should stay fresh-looking for several hours.)

1. touch of lace

Leave the damask tablecloth in the linen closet. An easier and more inviting alternative is to display each of your desserts (and stacks of plates) on its own paper doily.

2. paper and plastic

For the few offerings not meant to be eaten (oh-so-delicately) with the fingers, provide plastic forks and spoons. Set them out wrapped in cute polka-dot paper napkins tied up with a length of bakery string.

These easy-bake confections are far from cookie-cutter—not to mention a feast for the eyes. Store-bought treats make perfectly suitable sidekicks.

coconut pudding cake

hands-on time: 20 minutes • total time: 2 hours, 20 minutes (includes chilling)

- 1 3.4-ounce package instant vanilla pudding mix
- 2 pound cakes (store-bought or homemade)
- 1 cup heavy cream
- $1/2$ cup flaked sweetened coconut, toasted in a 350° F oven for 10 minutes

Prepare the pudding according to the package directions. Cover and refrigerate for at least 1 hour and up to 24 hours. Meanwhile, cut each pound cake in half crosswise. Slice each portion lengthwise twice to form 3 thin cake layers. Cover the bottom of an 8-inch-square baking pan with 4 of the layers. In a medium bowl, with an electric mixer on medium-high, beat the cream until soft peaks form. Gently fold the pudding into the whipped cream with a spatula. Spread 1 cup of the pudding mixture evenly over the cake in the baking pan. Repeat the layering 2 more times. Cover and refrigerate the cake for at least 1 hour and up to 24 hours. Sprinkle the top with the coconut just before serving. Serve cold.

hot chocolate cakes

hands-on time: 20 minutes • total time: 55 minutes

- 8 tablespoons (1 stick) unsalted butter, plus extra for coating
- 10 ounces semisweet chocolate, roughly chopped
- 4 large eggs
- 1 large egg yolk
- 1 teaspoon vanilla extract
- $1/4$ teaspoon kosher salt
- $1/2$ cup granulated sugar, plus extra for dusting
- 3 tablespoons all-purpose flour, plus extra for dusting
- $1/2$ cup mini marshmallows

Heat oven to 375° F. Generously butter, flour, and sugar eight 6-ounce ramekins or ovenproof coffee cups or mugs, tapping out any excess coatings. Wipe the rims clean and place on a baking sheet. Place the butter and chocolate in a large heatproof bowl set over a saucepan of simmering water (the bowl should not touch the water). Heat, stirring occasionally, until the butter and chocolate are melted and smooth. Remove from heat and let cool for 5 minutes.